SIMPLE STRATEGIES FOR BLOCK–SWAP QUILTS

LYNN RODDY BROWN

Martingale®
& COMPANY

Simple Strategies for Block-Swap Quilts
© 2009 by Lynn Roddy Brown

That Patchwork Place® is an imprint of
Martingale & Company®.

Martingale & Company
20205 144th Ave. NE
Woodinville, WA 98072-8478 USA
www.martingale-pub.com

Credits

President & CEO • Tom Wierzbicki
Editorial Director • Mary V. Green
Managing Editor • Tina Cook
Developmental Editor • Karen Costello Soltys
Technical Editor • Ellen Pahl
Copy Editor • Marcy Heffernan
Design Director • Stan Green
Production Manager • Regina Girard
Illustrators • Adrienne Smitke & Laurel Strand
Cover & Text Designer • Stan Green
Photographer • Brent Kane

Printed in China
13 12 11 10 09 08   8 7 6 5 4 3 2 1

Library of Congress Cataloging-in-Publication Data
Library of Congress Control Number: 2008037521

ISBN: 978-1-56477-858-1

MISSION STATEMENT

Dedicated to providing quality products and service
to inspire creativity.

DEDICATION

To all the families who, in a time of great sorrow, make the unselfish decision to save lives through organ donation.

ACKNOWLEDGMENTS

Thank you to the Blockbuilders of the Quilt Guild of Greater Houston for providing great trade blocks and years of inspiration. I have learned from all of you. Most important, you have given love and support during difficult times.

The following quilters have generously loaned quilts or given blocks. This book would not have happened without you. Thank you Elizabeth (Liz) Broussard, Rita Carter, Judy Fogelsong, Denise Goodman, Barbara Reynolds, Betty Rivers, Janice Thompson, Mary Tomlinson, and Fran Urquhart.

I would like to thank the staff at Martingale for doing your jobs so well. Special thanks go to editors Karen Costello Soltys and Ellen Pahl for so graciously putting up with me.

Finally, thanks go to my husband Bill for color consultations, photography, box packing, and patience. You have been there for me through good times and bad for over 40 years. I could not ask for a better husband.

CONTENTS

PROJECTS

INTRODUCTION

The scrap quilts in this book were all made using patchwork blocks acquired in trades. Making and trading identical sets of blocks is an efficient way to acquire many different blocks with a minimum of effort. It is also a wonderful way to get a greater variety of fabrics than a quilter would have using her own stash.

The quilt design process usually starts with an idea, a drawing, or a collection of fabric, and then after careful thought, the making of blocks. Designing with block trades is the opposite. You start with the blocks and then try to decide what can be done with what you have. Blocks from trades often go together easily for one-of-a-kind wonderful quilts. Other times they offer what I choose to call a challenge. This is when you are provided an opportunity to get out of your box, stretch your wings, experiment, and in the process, learn. To be successful, the quilter must keep an open mind. There are many possibilities. The

resulting quilt may not be what was planned but it can still be wonderful. Even if it isn't a favorite, it will keep someone warm.

I've found that successful trades have several things in common. Directions for trades must be very detailed and well written. Easy-to-piece blocks with straight-line sewing lead to more accurate construction. Trades resulting in the most finished quilts usually have a unifying element such as color, related fabrics, a common fabric, or consistent values.

For 10 years my bee has met monthly, traded blocks quarterly, eaten great food, laughed, argued, shared, and formed lasting friendships. It has been an amazing journey. Along the way I've learned about value, color, visual texture, and strategies for using many different types of blocks—even the "ugly" ones. I hope this book will inspire you and your quilting friends to start a journey of your very own.

UNDERSTANDING SCRAP QUILTS

I became interested in quilts during the early '70s. Many of the quilts featured in magazines at the time used just two or three fabrics. My husband's grandmother, known as Ga Ga to all who loved her, sent us a scrap quilt. I was very disappointed. I would have gladly provided fabric and a pattern for her to make a quilt like those in the magazines. But Ga Ga's quilt kept us warm for years—hidden under the bedspread! Each time I made the bed, I saw the quilt. Eventually I realized the quilt was a reflection of the personality of the maker and grew to love it. The well-worn quilt finally came out from under the bedspread!

Scrap quilts are about fabric, lots of fabric. In my opinion, the more fabrics, the better. I own a top, made by an unknown quilter, that uses random bits of fabric hand pieced onto newspaper. It is wonderful!! My own quilts are examples of my need for control. I like clear patterns, balanced color, and pleasing borders. After years of making scrap quilts, I am beginning to understand that it is often the imperfections that add life and energy to a quilt.

VALUE, VALUE, VALUE

In most quilts, the outline of the shapes is determined by color. Scrap quilts use many different fabrics in a wide range of colors. It is the relative darkness or lightness of the fabrics, or value, which determines the pattern.

Shown here are five fabrics arranged by value, from light to dark.

Some fabrics are difficult to use because they contain multiple values. It isn't the number of values that cause the problem as much as it is the proportion. The fabric at left contains almost even amounts of light, medium, and dark. The navy and beige checkerboard can't be described as light or dark. I used the black print with the bright motif in a pieced block; once it was sewn into the quilt, I was so unhappy with the results that I darkened the larger motif with a permanent marker.

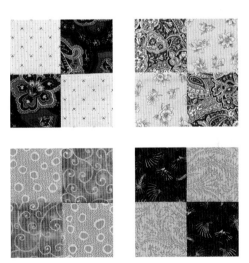

The Four Patch block at upper left uses a very light fabric and a very dark fabric. This gives the block strong clear lines. The block at upper right uses a medium light fabric and a medium fabric. It has less contrast but there is still a shift in value. The Four Patch block using pink and blue is more a contrast in color than value. In the example at lower right, the navy is darker, but the gold is so intense it becomes the focus of the block. The pattern in the lower two examples will probably be lost when sewn into a quilt and viewed from a distance.

Varying the value placement within a block can dramatically alter the pattern. When the blocks in a quilt are seen individually, as those in the Fox and Geese quilts on pages 81 and 85, I call them stand-alone blocks. Altering the value placement in a few of the blocks can add interest to a quilt. Shown below are blocks from the Churn Dash quilt "Zigzag" on page 63. The first example has the expected value placement: light background with medium/dark churn dash. Most of the blocks in the quilt should follow this pattern since they establish what the viewer expects to see. Altering the value placement in some of the blocks will make the viewer take another look. In the second block, values are in opposite positions within the block. In the third block, values are similar, causing the pattern to disappear when seen from a distance. Additional value changes can create what appears to be an entirely different block in the fourth example.

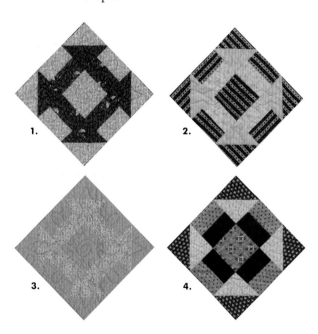

1. **Dark Churn Dash block with light background**
2. **Light Churn Dash block with dark background**
3. **Churn Dash block with similar values**
4. **Churn Dash block with a different pattern**

VISUAL TEXTURE

Most fabric has a pattern that is created by differences in value or color; stripes, dots, plaids, vines, and florals are all examples. An interesting scrap quilt needs a variety of prints that can be seen individually from a distance. This is known as visual texture. My chair is 15 feet from my design wall. I like to see visual texture from this distance.

Above are five red-and-white or red-and-cream prints from my stash. The first fabric is mostly white with tiny red stars. It is the proportion of white to red and the size of the motif that make this a very light fabric. In the second fabric, the motif is larger and more visible from a distance. The third fabric has wonderful diagonal lines that always add interest. The fourth and fifth prints have approximately the same proportion of color, but the fourth uses a regular pattern that stops the eye while the vine in the fifth example adds movement. When I began making scrap quilts several years ago, the fabric on the left would have been my choice. With each quilt, I've moved further to the right, including more of these highly textured fabrics.

Fabrics printed in one color family, but using more than one value of that color, are known as tone-on-tone fabrics. Many of these fabrics will appear solid from a distance. Solid fabrics and tone-on-tone fabrics that appear as solids tend to create flat areas. I avoid using this type of fabric unless it is used in the same position in all of the blocks. Tone-on-tone black fabrics were used in the Crossroads to Jericho blocks (pages 89 and 93). In this case they helped form strong lines across the surface.

In the tone-on-tone fabrics above, the left fabric in each pair has less visual texture.

TRADING BLOCKS

I'VE FOUND IN ALL OF LIFE IT IS OUR EXPECTATIONS THAT CAUSE OUR GREATEST DISAPPOINTMENTS.

If you expect to receive a set of perfectly made blocks that will result in the fabulous quilt you've envisioned, I guarantee you will be disappointed. If you go into a block trade with an open mind and consider it an opportunity to learn and grow as a quilter, you will be delighted.

When buying fabric, quilters usually choose the colors and patterns that they find most appealing. You might not agree with the fabric choices in the blocks you receive, but if the block is already made and in your hand, you are much more likely to give it a chance. This is where learning begins. The block that uses the "ugly" fabric you would never have bought, or the burnt orange you can't stand may be just the thing that turns a boring quilt into a great quilt. Taking home a bag of blocks made by other quilters should be thought of as a challenge. Attitude is everything.

ORGANIZING A GROUP

The first thing your group needs to do is determine what type of "rules" or "standards" you want. One small group that I am familiar with has very high standards for block construction. All of the members use the same brand of sewing machine and the same brand of rotary rulers. The number of blocks and the fabrics to be used are decided upon in advance. These trades result in predictable blocks with very few surprises. That group of six quilting friends has been meeting for years, and they are happy with their process and results.

My group is on the opposite end of the spectrum. There are usually 15 to 20 of us, and our standards are encouraged but rarely enforced. Instead we whine about the blocks we receive, and then sew them into wonderful, original quilts. Laughter, friendship, and support are our priorities along with sharing ideas, quilting tips, fabric, and food. For many years we operated without any written guidelines, but the six listed below have always been included in all pattern handouts.

- 100%-cotton fabric of quilt-store quality that has been washed
- 100%-cotton thread
- Accurately pieced blocks (not off by more than ⅛")
- Pressing as instructed on the handout
- Fabric selection as instructed on the handout

Any group needs a few rules or guidelines. After much trial and error we've discovered what works for us. In the fall of each year, members present blocks for consideration. Four are chosen for trading in March, June, September, and December of the following year. Handouts are made for each trade. We meet once a month for potluck lunch, quilting tips, visiting, and show and tell.

If you are starting a new group or are having problems with the quality of blocks, consider having piecing demonstrations. If space allows, members can bring their sewing machines and actually make blocks. The importance of accuracy and careful pressing can be emphasized in a helpful manner. This is much better for friendships than being critical of blocks brought to the trade. Since we meet monthly and trade quarterly there is time to discuss fabric choices and expectations. Beginning scrap quilters may need help understanding value and the importance of visual texture.

CHOOSING BLOCKS FOR SUCCESSFUL TRADES

I consider a block trade successful when the blocks come out of the bags and actually become quilts. Some of our trades have not produced finished quilts. Over the years, through trial and error, we have improved at selecting blocks.

Blocks that make good trades are those that can be set many different ways and work well with alternate blocks. We choose blocks that are easy to piece and range in size from 4" to 9" square. This encourages the making of many blocks and allows for more design possibilities. Fewer seams usually mean more accurate blocks. I find that if I've traded 200 easy-to-piece blocks, it isn't difficult to set aside the few that I don't like. If I've spent hours making 12 large, complicated blocks, my expectations for the trade will be high. This often results in disappointment.

Selecting blocks with a unifying element such as fabric type, color, or consistent values will result in more uniform sets of blocks that will go together easily. One successful trade called for tone-on-tone white fabrics and florals. This combination produced consistent values across the surface of the quilt and also included the unifying elements of color and fabric type.

Color: A very popular trade among my group was one of Four Patch blocks and half-square-triangle units made in blues and yellows. In almost all cases, the blues were darker than the yellows, providing more consistent values. Fran Urquhart's quilt "Sunshine on My Shoulders," above and on page 43, was made from this trade. Another group had wonderful results making blocks using different reds with tone-on-tone whites. You might consider red with green or pink with brown.

Consistent Values: It's important to use consistent values if the blocks are to form an overall pattern across the surface of the quilt. Blocks such as the Split Nine Patch must have consistent values. Before this trade, we brought fabrics to our meeting and discussed what would be considered light and medium/dark. If you are making a quilt of this type on your own, pull all of the fabrics you would like to use and sort them by value before you begin.

Several of our trades specify beige, ivory, tan, or ecru for backgrounds in an effort to get consistent values. Our acronym for this is BITE. We also use ICE for ivory, cream, and ecru.

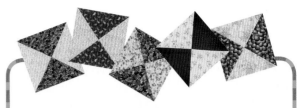

Common or Related Fabrics: Another approach is to use a common fabric or a type of fabric in all of the blocks. When we traded Churn Dash blocks, we required Civil War–era reproduction fabrics. The Internet trade of Bow Tie blocks on page 14 used a brand-name white with 1930s reproduction fabrics.

WHY I LOVE BLOCK TRADES

• I already have the fabric, and I will never use it all.

• I have a stash of fabric, a stash of blocks, and a stash of tops in addition to many completed quilts. The blocks I receive in trades are one step up from my fabric stash. They are a head start on a quilt, waiting there for me when and if I am inspired to use them. Longtime members of my group have bags and bags of blocks!!

• Making blocks is therapeutic.

• My blocks tend to be boring; blocks from others add spice to my quilts.

• Making blocks from trades is a learning experience. I am the quilter I am today only because I belonged to my trade group.

THE DETAILS

Read on for detailed information about how my group works. This may make it easier for your group to get started.

Sets of Blocks

A set is a group of 8 or 10 identical blocks all made from the same fabrics. Our blocks are simple and typically include just two or three fabrics. The number of blocks in a set is usually determined by how many blocks can be made from a fat quarter or full-width fabric strips. This allows members to use quick cutting and piecing methods when making the blocks. As an example, if you can make eight blocks from a quarter yard of fabric, that will be the number in the set; if you make 10 sets of eight you will have 80 blocks to trade.

The number of people trading might also determine the number in a set. If only six people are in the group, then six should be the maximum number in a set. Once a fabric is used in a set of blocks it isn't used again. A member may make as few sets or as many sets as she or he chooses.

HANDOUTS

The following information should be included in all handouts:

- Block or trade name
- Date when blocks will be traded
- Block illustration
- Block size, unfinished and finished
- Number of identical blocks in a set

Fabric:

- Specify prewashed 100%-cotton fabric of quilt-store quality
- Include color, print, or value as desired
- Specify a high contrast or low contrast for scrappy quilts
- Include type of fabric if appropriate, such as 1930s reproduction fabrics, Civil War reproductions, juvenile prints, brights, other reproductions, batiks, florals, plaids, etc.
- Indicate a common fabric to be bought and used by all members, such as muslin.

Other supplies:

- 100%-cotton thread
- Special rulers or other tools if needed
- Clear complete instructions for the efficient cutting, piecing, and pressing of a set of blocks

Distributing Blocks—aka The Trade

On the day of the trade, participants in my group sign in on a sheet of paper and indicate the number of block sets they are trading. The number of blocks in a set determines how the blocks are laid out for distribution. If there are eight blocks in a set, eight stacks will be arranged on each side of a fairly long table. We designate one person to be in charge of the distribution; two helpers assist in sorting the blocks. Each of the three people receives a pile of blocks belonging to a different member. Here is how we organize our trades:

1. Begin at the corner of the table with one member's blocks. Lay out the first set of eight blocks along one edge of the table. Place the second set of eight on the opposite side. Each helper follows so that one member's blocks will be alternated with those of two other members.

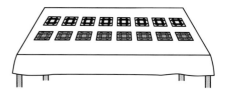

2. Continue around the table until each stack has eight blocks (or the number in the set). Place a piece of scrap paper on the top of each stack to separate the new sets. The paper needs to be large enough to stand out from the blocks so they can easily be separated later as needed.

3. Continue placing blocks around the table and adding papers after each set until all blocks are placed on the table.

Using this method, the stacks of blocks on one side of the table should be identical, but different from those on the opposite side of the table. When selecting sets to return to a participant, be sure to take them from both sides of the table. Each quilter takes home the same number of sets she brought.

In my group, we don't specify how many sets a member must make. There are advantages and disadvantages to this method. If one member makes 50 sets and the other members make between 5 and 10, there will be a larger proportion of blocks and fabric from the member who made 50. The advantage is that without a minimum number of sets, a quilter who may have been short on time that month can still participate. We are very flexible—if you bring it, we trade it.

Once the blocks are distributed, each person counts the blocks she received. When we are certain the trade has been done correctly, we often sort through our blocks and trade informally. Usually each person will get back a few of the blocks they brought.

ORGANIZING AND STORING BAGS OF BLOCKS

Members of my group generally use plastic zipper bags in the 1-gallon size for storing blocks. If that isn't large enough, any clear plastic bag can be used. Store bags in a box on a shelf, or use plastic crates. Plastic bags of blocks alone on a shelf will eventually become an avalanche, so it's best to keep them in a container of some sort.

DESIGNING WITH BLOCKS

I ALWAYS TRY TO MAKE MORE BLOCKS FOR A TRADE THAN I THINK I WILL NEED IN A QUILT. THIS GIVES ME MORE CHOICES AND ALSO EXTRA INSPIRATION.

The members of my block-trading group use different approaches when designing their quilts. What amazes me is that once the quilts are made I find them all appealing. Many use what I call the "Just Go For It" approach. I've never been able to do that. In the sections that follow, I cover some of the various design methods I use. I am sure there are many more, but these work for me.

JUST GO FOR IT

Some members simply use all of the blocks from a trade; they randomly sew them together and produce truly scrappy quilts. Others lay out the blocks, move a few around, and then sew them together. These quilts usually have energy and charm of their own. Judy Fogelsong's quilt, "Montana Scrappy," below and on page 39, is a wonderful example.

I like to make unique well-balanced quilts. I use a design wall and spend a considerable amount of time on the design process. After I finish making the quilts, they are thrown on a couch, put on a bed, or stuffed in a closet. I began to wonder why I spend so much time on design. I've decided there are two reasons: first, I enjoy the process; second, I'm afraid a great grandchild will hang one of my quilts. Since I've no idea which quilt will survive, they all better be wonderful!

I always try to make more blocks for a trade than I think I will need in a quilt. This gives me more choices and also extra inspiration. When I bring home a bag of blocks, I've no idea what the result will be. The only preconceived notion that I have is about size. Since the shortest person in my house is over 5'10", I usually make big quilts. I put the blocks on my design wall in a straight set and begin. Designing with already made blocks is a challenge for me, and that is what I have called my design approach, which I discuss further below.

DESIGN WALL

My design wall, which I consider a necessary tool, consists of two sheets of stiff insulation board covered with flannel. It was propped against my den wall for years. After my first book was published, my husband decided that maybe my quiltmaking was a serious endeavor. He put frames on the back of the insulation boards so only two nails are needed to hold them to the wall. If you don't have space for a permanent design wall, consider tacking up a flannel sheet. If you place the tacks where the wall meets the ceiling, the holes won't show. Another option is an inexpensive flannel backed plastic tablecloth. Painter's tape should hold it to the wall temporarily.

CONTROLLED

Before the trade for a set of blocks takes place, some quilters have already decided how they are going to use the blocks. For this approach to work, the block sets need to be very consistent and have one or more unifying elements. Below is the quilt I made from Bow Tie blocks obtained from an Internet trade. When researching Internet trades I found the directions to be very specific. For this trade, the background fabric was an exact shade of white made by a well-known manufacturer. The Bow Tie blocks were to be pieced from 1930s reproduction fabrics. When a trade is this controlled, you should be able to use all the blocks. Because Bow Tie blocks have a diagonal line, they can be set many different ways but the quilts will probably be very similar overall.

Bow Tie quilt made from a very controlled block trade.

CHALLENGE

Because I want a quilt with structure, and blocks from a trade are almost always inconsistent, design is a challenge for me. After a trade, I have a bag of blocks that are usually very different from blocks that I have made. Now what will I do with them?!

My first solution is to sort, either by color, intensity, visual texture, value, or anything else that works.

Sorting, Setting Aside, and Adding Blocks

When I was a beginning quilter, sampler quilts were popular. I stood in a show and asked an experienced quilter how in the world she knew which blocks would go well together. She said, "I just make lots of blocks, and then see which ones look best." This one comment opened up a whole new world for me.

When I bring home a new bag of blocks, I start by putting them on my design wall in a straight set. I step back, study the blocks and then begin sorting. Sometimes I feel I'm looking at completely unrelated blocks. I set aside the blocks that don't seem to fit my vision for the quilt. Often I will put as much as 30% of a trade back in the bag. With the first group of blocks I try to make the quilt that comes to mind first. Sometimes this works and sometimes it doesn't. Remember, an open mind is a must. Lately I've been using the blocks that were set aside and making what I like to call my second chance quilts. This is when the fun begins. Will I be able to make the left over blocks work well together?

Often I will get a block in a trade that is such an inspiration it will shift the direction of the quilt. I will go through my stash and look for similar fabrics and make more blocks. I have found that an odd number of a strong color or pattern works best. Three, five, or seven blocks seem to keep the eye moving. Sometimes it is necessary to make a quilt store run to search for more of that wonderful color or pattern.

If you find it upsetting not to use all of the blocks, remember that they can be pieced into the backing or become the start of a wonderful scrappy sampler quilt. If all else fails, they can be sold in a booth at a quilt show some day. Someone else will love them.

SETTING ALTERNATIVES

After my first look at a group of blocks in a straight setting, I will try them on point. This often creates diagonal lines, which keeps the viewer's eye moving across the surface and makes for a more interesting quilt.

Alternate Blocks

If blocks don't seem to go together, separating them with an alternate block often helps. This is also an easy way to make a larger quilt. Since alternate blocks will be as much as half of the blocks, they can also cause a shift in mood. If blocks need to be calmed down, add alternate blocks in grayed tones. Bright alternate blocks can perk up a boring group of blocks.

Adding alternate blocks is also a way to shift color. If you want a blue quilt, add alternate blocks in a blue fabric that you really like.

Fran Urquhart's "Civil War and Blue" is a good example of using alternate blocks to bring out one particular color.

Sashing

Sashing is another way to separate blocks and make a larger quilt. I've found a medium-value or a striped fabric often works well. Since the blocks usually use dark and light values, a medium-value sashing will give a clear line. Striped fabric has two values close together, which gives visual texture to clearly separate the blocks.

INTENSITY OF COLOR

When blocks don't seem to go together, I find the problem is often the intensity of the colors. If I am making a clear bright children's quilt, a grayed purple will detract from the rest of the blocks. If most of the blocks are Civil War reproduction fabrics, lime green might not be what is needed. Even when a group of blocks is based on color, you may have blocks you don't like.

My group traded half-square-triangle units and four-patch units in blue and yellow. The blues could go from light blue to teal and on to dark blue. The yellow could go from light yellow to gold. Small amounts of other colors were allowed as long as the blocks "read" blue and yellow. The "Just Go For It" group took everything, sewed it together, and was happy

with their quilts. Fran Urquhart's "Sunshine on My Shoulders" on page 43 is an example.

My friend Mary Tomlinson had other ideas. When Mary participated in the trade, she had pale blues and soft yellows in mind. The blocks didn't meet her expectations. She sorted the blocks by intensity of color and made three quilts, shown below.

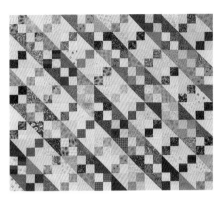

For one quilt, Mary Tomlinson used the pale colors. This would be wonderful for a baby.

For her second quilt, Mary grouped the darkest blues and golds. This isn't Mary's favorite, but I think it works.

The third quilt made wonderful use of the remaining half-square triangles.

STRUCTURE

Most scrap quilts have some type of structure. They are usually made from sets of blocks in which structure or pattern is determined by value. Blocks with inconsistent values are often difficult to use in this type of quilt. Sometimes if these blocks are sorted by value, they can then be arranged to form a pattern.

"Barn Raising" is an example of a quilt with an overall pattern using blocks with consistent values.

I had a bag of Hourglass blocks that had been around for years. The directions for the trade were to use a light and a dark in each block to provide strong contrast. Some of the blocks actually did have strong contrast. The others used a medium with a darker fabric or a medium with a lighter fabric and some seemed to have no contrast at all. There was also a tremendous variation in visual texture. Denise Goodman, one member of our group, used a few of hers as an alternate block with Nine Patch blocks in "Country Cousins" on page 49, but the rest of us allowed our blocks to languish in the bags.

I challenged myself to do something with the blocks. I made a rule that I would use every block in the bag, and I couldn't add more blocks. I had to use exactly what I had. I opened the bag, and after much thought and sorting, I decided there was no way I could use all the blocks in the same quilt. I first selected all the low-contrast blocks and arranged them on the design wall. The next step was to pick out the high-contrast blocks and place them in another

area of the wall. The remaining blocks were placed at the lower right where I kept hoping they would disappear.

As I worked, blocks would move from one area of the wall to another. I was looking for the best possible combinations. I was finally happy with the first two groups which are shown below.

Blocks using light with medium and medium with dark create low contrast.

Blocks using very light with dark result in very high contrast.

Now what in the world would I do with the remaining blocks? Randomly placed they had no appeal. These blocks had been rejected for low-contrast, intense colors or extreme textures. Some were very poorly made. I started taking a few of the blocks apart and resewing them. They should have been 6½" unfinished. Even after resewing some were off more than ¼". I finally pressed all the blocks and trimmed them to an unfinished size of 6". After much squinting to see values, I realized I had four blocks with white backgrounds. I decided these could be used as star points for an Ohio Star. I placed low-contrast blocks in the areas where one fabric would normally be used to form the star pattern. I then tried many different positions for the remaining blocks. It took me a long time to find a structure that pleased me. In the end this sample became one of my favorites because every time I look I see something different.

Blocks with low contrast, strong colors, and extreme textures are arranged to create a pattern.

I was so excited about my success with the Hourglass blocks that I talked Rita Carter, another member of our group, into trading her Hourglass blocks for another bag of my unused blocks. Making the samples gave me the confidence to tackle a large quilt that would use a variety of values within the blocks. "Order Out of Chaos" on page 45 was the result. Rita's blocks included four identical blocks I was able to use for the center. As I worked outward and wanted to repeat rows based on value, I made more blocks using the needed values. "Second Chance" on page 53 uses most, but not all, of the leftover blocks. There are a few still in the bag.

UNDERLYING STRUCTURE

This is the term I use when there is a structure, but it is not readily apparent. In some cases you may never notice it, but I feel it is often what holds a quilt together and makes it appealing. If you go back to the first Hourglass example on page 44 and tip the page or squint your eyes until the color dims, you may see a secondary pattern. I alternated blocks with lighter backgrounds with blocks that had medium backgrounds. The alternate pattern forms where similar values touch.

When working with the second set of Hourglass blocks I noticed lots of red. I sorted the blocks and found 12 of the 25 blocks were red or a variation of red. I alternated these blocks with the other blocks. This was an easy way to scatter the red blocks and keep them from touching.

I made the Fox and Geese quilts on pages 81 and 85 after making "Order Out of Chaos." I began thinking more about using some type of structure in my design process. In "Goose the Fox" the blocks with light backgrounds are alternated in diagonal rows with blocks that have medium to dark backgrounds. In "Orange Can Be Wonderful" I kept rearranging blocks and couldn't seem to make the quilt work. I finally pulled out eight blocks that I felt were "heavier" than the others. These blocks have darker backgrounds and stronger colors. I used these blocks across the top, across the bottom, and up the middle. I could still move blocks but these eight blocks had to stay in one of these positions. Using structure, whether it is obvious or underlying, makes it easier for me to create arrangements that I find pleasing.

QUILTMAKING TECHNIQUES

IN THIS SECTION I'VE INCLUDED A FEW OF MY FAVORITE TECHNIQUES AND HELPFUL HINTS. CHECK OUT SOME OF THE MANY EXCELLENT QUILTING BOOKS AT YOUR LOCAL QUILT SHOP IF YOU'RE A BEGINNER AND NEED FURTHER INFORMATION ABOUT A SPECIFIC TOPIC.

PRESSING

After sewing each seam, press it flat as it was sewn to set the seam; then press the seam allowance open or to one side before adding the next piece. Usually seam allowances are pressed to one side, toward the darker fabric. In the project instructions, I suggest that you press many of the seam allowances open. I do this because I machine quilt all my quilts, and pressing the seam allowances open creates a smoother, flatter surface with less skipping and thread breakage. I use quilting patterns that cross over the seams, thereby stabilizing and holding them together. If you're planning to outline the quilt patches either by hand or machine—or if you're planning to tie the quilt—you might want to press all the seam allowances to the side.

HALF-SQUARE-TRIANGLE UNITS

I begin with paired squares of fabric to make either two or eight identical half-square-triangle units at once. I always make half-square-triangle units slightly oversized, and then trim them to the correct size.

1. Cut squares the size indicated in the pattern, and then pair your fabrics, choosing the light and dark fabric that you want for the half-square-triangle unit.

2. Using the two squares that will be sewn together, lay the first fabric, right side up, on the ironing board. Spray evenly with spray starch.

3. Lay the second fabric, right side down, on top of the first, aligning the edges, and press well. The paired fabrics should now be smooth, crisp, lightly stuck together, and ready to cut.

4. Cut the square in half on the diagonal using a ruler and rotary cutter. I like to place one pin in the units to hold the pieces together before removing them from the cutting mat.

SQUARES FOR PAIRS

To determine the size to cut squares, use these formulas:
- **Two identical half-square triangles:** Add 1¼" to the desired finished size and cut your original squares to that size. (For 3" half-square-triangle units, cut 2 squares 4¼" x 4¼".)
- **Eight identical half-square triangles:** Add 1" to the desired finished size and multiply by 2; cut your original squares to that size. (For 3" half-square-triangle units, cut 2 squares, 8" x 8".)

Making Two Identical Units

1. Make paired fabrics as described in "Half-Square-Triangle Units" at left.

2. Sew the diagonal seams and cut the units apart. Press to set the seam, and then press the seam allowance toward the darker fabric.

3. Trim the units, referring to "Squaring Up Units" on page 19.

Making Eight Identical Units

1. Make paired fabrics as described in "Half-Square-Triangle Units" at left.

2. Sew the diagonal seams and cut the units apart.

3. Align a ruler with the line of stitching and the triangle point. Cut. Repeat for both units to make four triangles.

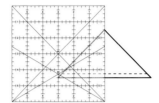
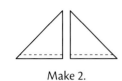

Make 2.

4. Start at the right-angle corner of each of the units from step 3 and stitch the cut edge as shown. The stitches will cross at the corner.

Make 4.

5. Align a ruler with the unsewn edge and the point of the units from step 4 and cut as shown. You will have eight identical half-square triangles. Press to set the seams, and then press the seam allowances toward the dark fabric.

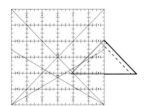

Make 8.

6. Trim the units, referring to "Squaring Up Units" at right.

Squaring Up Units

1. Use a small, square ruler with a diagonal line to trim and square up each half-square triangle. Position the diagonal line on the seam of the unit with the fabric extending just beyond the edge of the ruler. Trim the two adjacent sides.

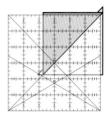
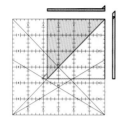

2. Rotate the unit and position the ruler so that the two trimmed edges of the unit are on the ruler lines for the required size. Trim the excess fabric from the remaining two sides.

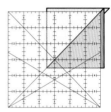
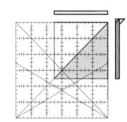

SQUARE-IN-A-SQUARE UNITS

Square-in-a-square units have a center square with a triangle attached to each of the four sides, resulting in a second, larger pieced square. Units are much more accurate if the triangles are cut oversized, added to the four sides of the square, and then trimmed.

1. Fold the triangles in half right side out and lightly press to mark the center of each long side. Fold the block in half with right side in and press the edges to mark the centers. Fold the block the opposite way right side in and mark the center of the other two block edges. Use the creases to align a triangle with the center of each block edge. Sew triangles to two opposite sides of the block. Press the seam allowances toward the triangles and trim the triangle points.

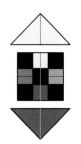
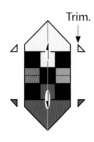

Trim.

2. Sew triangles to the remaining sides of the units. Press toward the triangles.

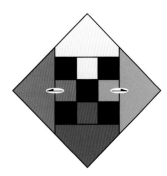

3. Place the pieced unit under a square ruler. Align the ¼" line on the ruler with the top and right points of the center square. Trim the right side and top of the block. Rotate the block 180º and trim the two remaining sides in the same manner.

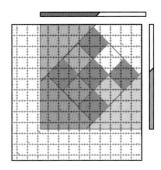

SQUARING UP BLOCKS

When blocks have been traded they often aren't the same size. If a block is less than ⅛" off—too large or too small—I will make adjustments when piecing the blocks together. If blocks are too large and they don't have points on the edges, they can often be squared to the correct size.

1. Carefully press the block. Look for seam allowances that are obviously too small. Taking in one or more of the seam allowances may solve the problem.

2. Find the center of the block. Take the desired unfinished size of the block and divide by 2. If the unfinished size is 6½" then half would be 3¼". Align the ruler 3¼" mark with the center of the block. Trim away the excess that extends beyond the top and the right sides of the ruler. Rotate the block 180°, so that the trimmed edges are under the ruler on the marks

for the desired block size. In this case it would be 6½". Remember, you must trim equal amounts from all four sides.

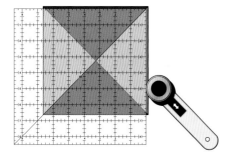

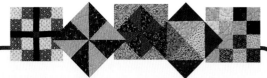

TIPS FOR FITTING BLOCKS TOGETHER

If you've traded blocks and they're not all quite the same size, here are some tips for making them fit together easier:

• Be sure the seam allowances are correctly pressed. The blocks may be too small because of pressed-in tucks. Re-press the blocks if necessary.

• Use a steam iron to square up and shrink blocks that are too large and to stretch blocks that are too small.

• Place the larger block on the bottom when joining to a smaller block. The feed dogs will help to ease the extra fabric in.

• If the size difference is less than ⅛", center the smaller block on the larger block.

• If the size difference is greater than ¼", don't use the block unless you remake it. Remember, it's okay to reject a block.

QUILT SETS

A quilt set or setting is how the blocks in a quilt are arranged. The quilts in this book are set in one of three different ways—straight, diagonal, or in vertical rows. You can always choose a different setting from the one shown in the photograph.

Whenever there are sashing strips or plain alternate blocks in a quilt setting, I suggest that you wait until all the blocks are sewn before cutting those elements of the quilt. Your blocks may vary from the exact size by ⅛" or more due to slight differences in cutting and piecing. Measure your blocks and then cut those pieces to fit your blocks. Your quilt will go together much easier this way.

Straight Sets

In straight sets, blocks are simply sewn together into horizontal rows. The rows are joined to complete the top. When joining the rows, be sure to carefully match the vertical seams of each row with the next. I pin all of these intersections.

Vertical Strippy Sets

Betty River's quilts, "UFO Complete" on page 77 and "Zigzag" on page 63, are examples of strippy sets. Blocks are sewn together into panels to create vertical rows.

Diagonal Sets

In diagonal sets, the blocks are placed on point. This requires side setting triangles and corner setting triangles. Throughout the project instructions, the side and corner setting triangles are cut larger than necessary. This allows for minor piecing errors and gives you an extra margin of insurance.

1. Sew the blocks together in diagonal rows, adding the side setting triangles to the ends. To add the side setting triangles, first align the corners. Allow the point of the triangle to extend beyond the block as shown. Sew the seam, press toward the triangle, and then trim the point. Sew the diagonal rows together. Add the corner triangles last.

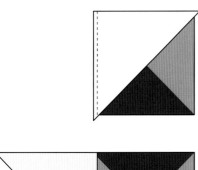

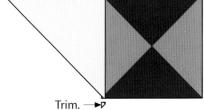

Trim. ➡

2. Trim the edges of the quilt top to ¼" away from the block points before adding borders. Align the ¼" mark of a rotary ruler on the block points as shown.

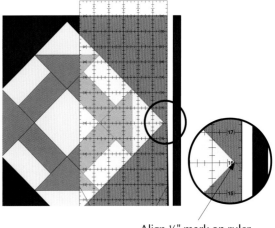

Align ¼" mark on ruler
with block point. Trim.

BORDERS

Many of the quilts in this book have a narrow inner border and a wider outer border. If the outer border is wider than 3", I like to cut it on the lengthwise grain. This requires more fabric, but has the advantage of being less stretchy than the crosswise grain. Borders cut on the lengthwise grain help keep the quilt square and flat. The inner borders are cut from the crosswise grain and are sewn together end to end, with a straight or diagonal seam, to get the required length. I prefer a diagonal seam because I think it is less noticeable. If I use a striped fabric, I match the stripe and join the strips with a straight seam. Press all border seam allowances open, whether they are straight or diagonal.

Borders with Butted Corners

1. Lay the quilt out on a smooth surface. Measure lengthwise through the middle. Use this measurement to cut side borders. Mark the middle and quarter points of the borders.

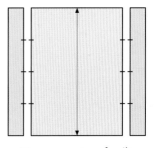

Measure center of quilt,
top to bottom.

2. Place the borders on the quilt, right sides together, matching the ends, quarter points, and middle. Pin carefully. If the edges of the quilt have stretched so that they're longer than the borders, take the quilt top, with the pinned border attached, to the ironing board. With the border underneath and the quilt on top, use a steam iron until the quilt can be eased to fit the border. Add additional pins before removing the quilt from the ironing board.

3. Stitch the border to the quilt, with the pieced side on top (facing up). This allows you to see any triangle points and helps prevent seam allowances from flipping. A walking foot is a tremendous help when sewing borders. Press the seam allowances toward the border.

4. Measure the width of the quilt top across the middle, including the side borders just added. Cut the borders to this length and sew them to the top and bottom as you did the sides.

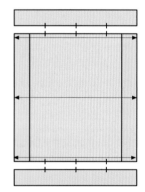

Measure center of quilt, side to side, including border strips.

5. Repeat the steps to add any additional borders.

Borders with Corner Squares

1. Lay the quilt out on a smooth surface. Measure lengthwise through the middle. Use this measurement to cut the side borders. Measure the width of the quilt through the center. Use this measurement to cut the top and bottom borders. Mark the middle and quarter points of all borders.

2. Position the side borders on the quilt top, right sides together, matching the ends, quarter points, and middle. Stitch the side borders to the quilt top, with the pieced side on top (facing up). Press toward the borders.

3. Sew a corner square to each end of the top and bottom border strips. Sew these to the quilt top and bottom, easing as necessary.

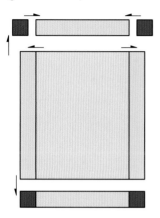

Borders with Mitered Corners

1. Measure the length and width of your quilt through the center.

2. To determine the border lengths, add twice the width of the borders plus 4" to the quilt measurements from step 1. If you are mitering multiple borders, sew all of the borders together first, pressing the seam allowances open. Use the width of the multiple borders in your calculation.

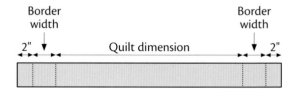

3. Mark the centers of the borders. Use the length and width measurements from step 1 to mark the ends of the borders. Mark the quilt centers. On the wrong side of the quilt top, mark a dot ¼" in from both edges of all four corners.

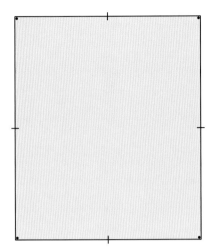

4. With right sides together, pin one border in place, matching the center and ends of the quilt and border. To join the border to the top, begin stitching one stitch out from the dot; backstitch after two or three forward stitches. Stitch forward, toward the next corner. Stop one stitch before you reach the dot on the corner and backstitch. Press the seam allowance toward the border. Add the remaining borders in the same manner.

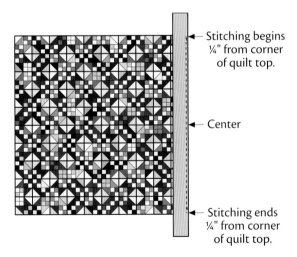

Stitching begins ¼" from corner of quilt top.

Center

Stitching ends ¼" from corner of quilt top.

5. To sew the mitered corners, first place the quilt on an ironing board. Layer the top border over the side border. Fold the top border piece at a 45º angle to the bottom piece, matching the long raw edges and placing right sides together. If you are using multiple borders, put pins through the seams, making sure

they line up. Use a square ruler with a diagonal line to check the accuracy of the fold; press.

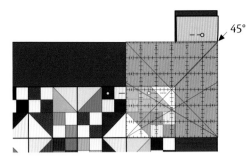

Align the fold under the ruler's 45° angle.

6. Fold the two border pieces right sides together. Pin the end and edges where necessary. Draw a pencil line on the crease so you can see where to sew. Starting one stitch out from the end of the previous stitching line, stitch on the crease to the outside edge. Repeat for all four corners. Check on the right side to see that the miters are sewn correctly. Trim the excess fabric, leaving a ¼" seam allowance. Press the seam allowances open.

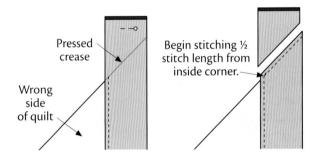

Pressed crease

Wrong side of quilt

Begin stitching ½ stitch length from inside corner.

LAYERING AND BASTING

Instructions with each project will tell you how to piece the backing. After piecing, trim the backing to 4" larger than your quilt top on all sides. The batting should also be at least 4" larger all around.

I machine quilt and use 1" safety pins to baste. If you plan to hand quilt, baste with thread in a grid about every 6". Before basting, make sure the backing and top are well pressed. I throw my batting in the clothes dryer on low heat for a few minutes to remove wrinkles.

Secure the backing, right side down, to a table with masking tape or binder clips. Lay the batting out on top of the backing, smoothing out any wrinkles. Then add the quilt top and smooth out any wrinkles. Before pinning, decide where the quilting lines will go and avoid placing pins there. If I plan to cross the middle of a block, I'll pin the edges of the block. Pin along the sides of the inner borders to keep them straight. Place pins about a fist width apart.

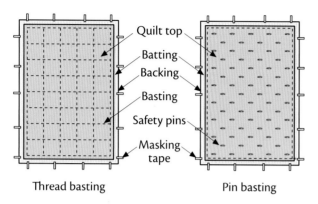

Quilt top
Batting
Backing
Basting
Safety pins
Masking tape

Thread basting   Pin basting

BINDING

Bindings can be cut on the bias or on the straight of grain. In my experience, bias bindings wear longer and the hand sewing seems easier. Striped fabrics or plaids cut on the bias make a lovely binding. Straight-grain bindings, however, use less fabric, stretch less, and are easier to cut. Straight-grain bindings will help hold a wall hanging square.

The cutting instructions for each quilt provide the number of straight-grain strips to cut for binding. If I've used a striped fabric or a plaid cut on the bias, I've included the yardage needed for bias strips and the total number of inches needed as well. I cut my strips 2½" wide for a ⅜" finished binding. For bias strips, cut at a 45° angle across the center of the fabric to get the longest strips possible.

1. Join the binding strips with diagonal seams. Press the seam allowances open. Fold the binding lengthwise, wrong sides together, and press.

2. I sew with a seam gauge and trim the quilt before attaching the binding. First stitch around the entire quilt ⅛" from the edge of the quilt top using a walking foot.

3. Use a large, square ruler and a long ruler to trim the quilt and make sure that the corners are square. Align the rulers with the inner border or a seam in the patchwork. If a quilt has a plain border, I trim to the edge of the fabric. If your quilt has blocks along the outer edge, such as "Churned-Up Geese" on page 67, first make sure the corner blocks are square. If they

aren't, pin them square and use steam to set them. Since I use a ⅜" seam allowance to attach the binding, I trim ⅛" away from the edge of the blocks.

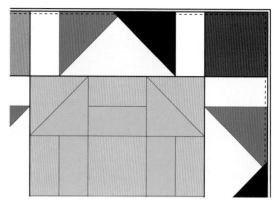

Stitch ⅛" in from the edge of the quilt top.
Trim backing and batting ⅛" beyond quilt top edge.

4. To avoid having a binding seam fall at a corner of the quilt, place the binding around the quilt using a few pins. I start on the top edge and position the binding so that the first binding seam will be sewn before I turn the upper-right corner. I continue placing the binding around the entire quilt, folding it at the quilt corners. If a binding seam hits a corner of the quilt, I reposition the entire binding. When I'm sure the binding is starting in the correct position, I remove all the pins except the one at the starting point.

5. Begin stitching 6" from the start of the binding using a ⅜" seam allowance. Bring the bobbin thread up and stitch a few inches. As you approach the first corner, stop the machine and use a small ruler to mark ⅜" from the raw edge of the corner. Sew to the mark and backstitch three stitches.

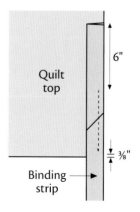

Quilt top

6"

Binding strip

⅜"

6. Remove the quilt from the machine. Fold the binding up so that it is aligned with the next edge and the fold creates a 45° angle with the corner. Turn the binding down to make a fold in the binding that is in line with the upper raw edge of the quilt top. Pin. Be absolutely sure that the fold doesn't extend beyond the quilt top. Put the quilt back under the presser foot. Lower the needle about ⅛" away from the top fold, pull up the bobbin thread, sew three stitches, backstitch three stitches, and then continue sewing until you approach the next corner. Stop ⅜" from the corner and repeat the mitering process at each corner.

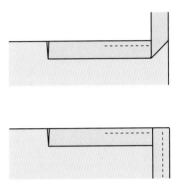

7. When stitching the last side, stop approximately 12" from the starting point. Remove the quilt from the machine. Fold the unstitched binding edges back on themselves so they just meet in the middle over the unsewn area of the quilt top. Press the folds.

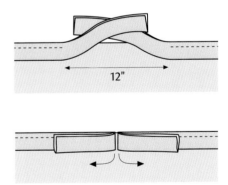

8. The easiest way to join the binding ends is to trim the ends straight across, ¼" out from the fold lines. Sew the seam. Press the seam allowance open. Re-press the binding. Make certain the binding fits the unsewn area and finish sewing it to the quilt.

9. Turn the binding to the back of the quilt and hand sew it in place using thread that matches the binding. Miter the corners as shown.

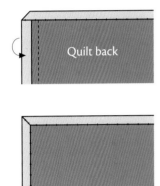

PINWHEELS BOTH WAYS
Made by Lynn Roddy Brown.
Finished quilt: 60" x 77" • Finished block: 12" x 12" • Number of blocks: 18

PINWHEELS BOTH WAYS

I first saw this dynamic quilt setting in Joan Hanson's book *Sensational Settings*. Notice that the pinwheels are set on point in 12 blocks and set straight in 6. The blocks are framed and then squared to a consistent size; this is a useful technique when all the blocks aren't exactly the same size.

The six pinwheels that are set straight have very strong colors without obvious differences in value. These blocks were from the same trade as those used in "Pinwheel Nine Patch" on page 31. I felt they wouldn't work well in that quilt due to the strong colors. Sometimes making odd blocks the main focus can be a solution.

MATERIALS

All yardages are based on 42"-wide fabric unless otherwise noted.

1⅞ yards of dark purple print for border and binding

1⅓ yards of pink floral for framing blocks and setting triangles

1⅛ yards of green dotted fabric for block frames

1 yard *total* of medium/dark scraps for Pinwheel blocks

1 yard *total* of light scraps for Pinwheel blocks

⅞ yard of medium purple striped fabric for setting triangles

5¼ yards of fabric for backing*

68" x 85" piece of batting

12½" square ruler

*Consider piecing extra half-square-triangle units or fabric strips to make a length of 68". Piece this into the crosswise seam; using this method you would need 4¼ yards of backing fabric.

CUTTING

All measurements include ¼"-wide seam allowances.

From the medium/dark scraps cut:

18 matching pairs of squares, 5¼" x 5¼"

From the light scraps cut:

18 matching pairs of squares, 5¼" x 5¼"

From the green dotted fabric*, cut:

14 strips, 2½" x 42"; crosscut into:
    24 strips, 2½" x 8½"
    24 strips, 2½" x 12½"

From the pink floral, cut:

3 squares, 12¾" x 12¾" along one selvage edge; cut each square twice diagonally to yield 12 side triangles (2 are extra).

12 squares, 7½" x 7½"; cut each square once diagonally to yield 24 framing triangles.

1 square, 5½" x 5½"; cut twice diagonally to yield 4 corner triangles.

From the medium purple striped fabric**, cut:

8 strips, 3¼" x 42"; crosscut into:
    10 strips, 3¼" x 20"
    8 strips, 3¼" x 12"

From the dark purple print, cut:

8 strips, 4¾" x 42"
8 strips, 2½" x 42"

*Wait to cut these framing strips until after the Pinwheel blocks are made.

** If you are using a striped fabric, cut the eight 3¼" x 12" strips individually starting on the same color/width stripe. Pay close attention if the stripes are irregular.

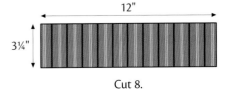

Cut 8.

MAKING THE BLOCKS

For each block you will need two matching light 5¼"
squares and two matching medium/dark 5¼" squares.

1. Pair each pair of light squares with a pair of
medium/dark squares. Referring to "Half-Square-
Triangle Units" on page 18, make two identical pieced
squares from each. Press the seam allowances toward
the medium/dark fabric and trim completed units to
4½" square.

2. Lay out the units as shown. Make certain the
light and medium/dark fabrics are in the correct
positions. Sew the units together in rows; press the
seam allowances open. Join the rows; press the seam
allowances open.

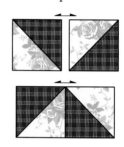

3. Repeat steps 1 and 2 to make a total of 18 blocks.
The Pinwheel blocks should measure 8½" x 8½". If
any are too large, refer to "Squaring Up Blocks" on
page 20.

ADDING FRAMING STRIPS AND TRIANGLES

1. Cut framing strips from the green dotted fabric
as directed in the cutting list on page 27. If you have
blocks smaller than 8½", cut the framing strips
2¾" wide.

2. Sew 8½"-long framing strips to opposite sides of 12
Pinwheel blocks. Press the seam allowances toward
the framing strips. Sew 12½"-long framing strips to
the remaining sides of the 12 units. Press the seam
allowances toward the framing strips. The blocks
should measure 12½" square.

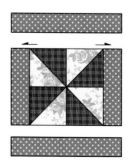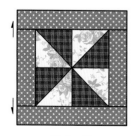

Make 12.

3. Fold the pink floral 7½" triangles in half and lightly
press to mark the center of each long side. Use the
crease to align the triangle with the center seam of the
block. Sew triangles to two opposite sides of the six
unframed blocks. Press the seam allowances toward
the triangles and trim.

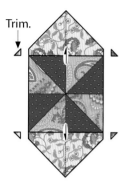

Trim.

4. Sew framing triangles to the remaining sides of the
units; press toward the triangles.

Make 6.

5. Refer to "Squaring Up Blocks" on page 20. Center-
ing the pinwheel, square up the blocks to 12½" x 12½".
Pinwheels should float within the block.

MAKING SETTING TRIANGLES

1. Fold the 10 purple striped 3¼" x 20" strips in half,
with right sides together. Lightly press to mark the
centers of each long side. Fold 10 of the pink floral
12¾" setting triangles right side out. Lightly press to
mark the center of each long edge. Lay each triangle

on a strip, right sides together, matching the center creases. Stitch as shown. Press the seam allowances toward the triangles.

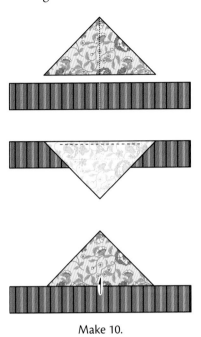

Make 10.

2. Lay a ruler along one pieced triangle edge aligning it as shown and trim the excess purple fabric. Repeat for the opposite side. The long edge of the pieced triangle should measure between 18¼" and 18½".

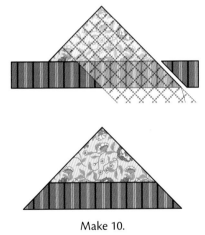

Make 10.

3. On the wrong side of a pink floral 5½" triangle, mark a dot ¼" in from both edges of the corner. Choose a stripe at least 3½" from an end. Use a pin to align the dot with the stripe. Pin the triangle to the strip. Start stitching one stitch away from the dot and continue to the end of the triangle as shown; press toward the striped fabric.

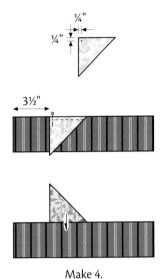

Make 4.

4. Using a second strip, align the triangle dot with the identical stripe used in step 4; pin. Start stitching one stitch away from the dot and continue to the end of the triangle. Stitch one stitch away from the dot to the end of the triangle; press toward the striped fabric.

5. Place the unit face up on the ironing board. Fold the top strip over the bottom strip at a 45° angle. The stripes should match. Adjust if necessary. Pin the strip ends; press.

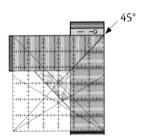

6. Fold the two strips right sides together. The stripes of the two pieces should match. Using the crease as your stitching line, machine baste, beginning one stitch away from the dot and sewing to the edge of the strips. Check to see if the stripes match; remove the stitches, pin, and resew if adjustments need to be made. If the stripes align, reset the stitch length to normal and stitch over the line a second time. Trim the excess fabric, leaving a ¼" seam allowance. Press the seam allowance open.

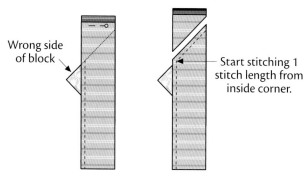

7. Align a ruler with the bottom edge of the pink triangle. Trim as shown. The long side of the pieced triangle should measure between 13¼" and 13½". Repeat steps 3–7 to make three additional corner setting triangles.

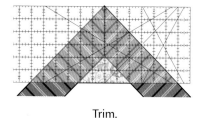

Trim.

Make 4.

ASSEMBLING THE QUILT TOP

1. Referring to the quilt assembly diagram, arrange the blocks and the side setting triangles into diagonal rows on a design wall.

2. Sew the blocks and side setting triangles together into rows, referring to "Diagonal Sets" on page 21. Press the seam allowances away from the triangle-framed blocks.

3. Join the rows. Press the seam allowances open. Add the corner setting triangles and press outward. Trim the quilt on all four sides, leaving a ¼" seam allowance beyond the block points.

4. For each border, sew two dark purple 4¾" strips together end to end using a diagonal seam. Press the seam allowances open.

5. Add the side borders, referring to "Borders with Butted Corners" on page 21. Press the seam allowance toward the borders. Add the top and bottom borders and press the seam allowances toward the borders.

FINISHING THE QUILT

1. Cut the backing fabric across the grain into two equal pieces. Remove the selvages. Sew these pieces together along the lengthwise grain to create the quilt back. Press the seam allowance open. The seam will run vertically on the quilt.

2. Refer to "Layering and Basting" on page 23; hand or machine quilt as desired.

3. Use the dark purple 2½" strips to bind the quilt, referring to "Binding" on page 24.

4. Make and attach a label to your quilt.

HALF-SQUARE-TRIANGLE UNITS FOR TRADES

Finished size: 4" x 4" • Yield: 8

From one light fabric, cut:
1 square, 10" x 10"

From one medium to dark fabric, cut:
1 square: 10" x 10"

Refer to "Half-Square-Triangle Units" on page 18 to make eight identical units. After stitching and cutting them apart, trim each unit to 4½" x 4½". My group traded these in groups of four. Connect four identical units together with a pin or tack with thread.

ALTERNATE BLOCK LAYOUT

PINWHEEL NINE PATCH

Made by Lynn Roddy Brown.
Finished quilt: 65" x 65"
Finished block: 16" x 16"

This was the first quilt I made using the half-square-triangle units. I sorted the units by color and placed them on my design wall in groups of four. I originally planned to make 12 blocks, but as I moved the blocks from group to group I was only happy with nine of the combinations. Having more blocks than you need encourages you to try many possibilities and usually results in a more pleasing quilt. The blocks that I didn't use in this quilt were later stitched into "Pinwheels Both Ways."

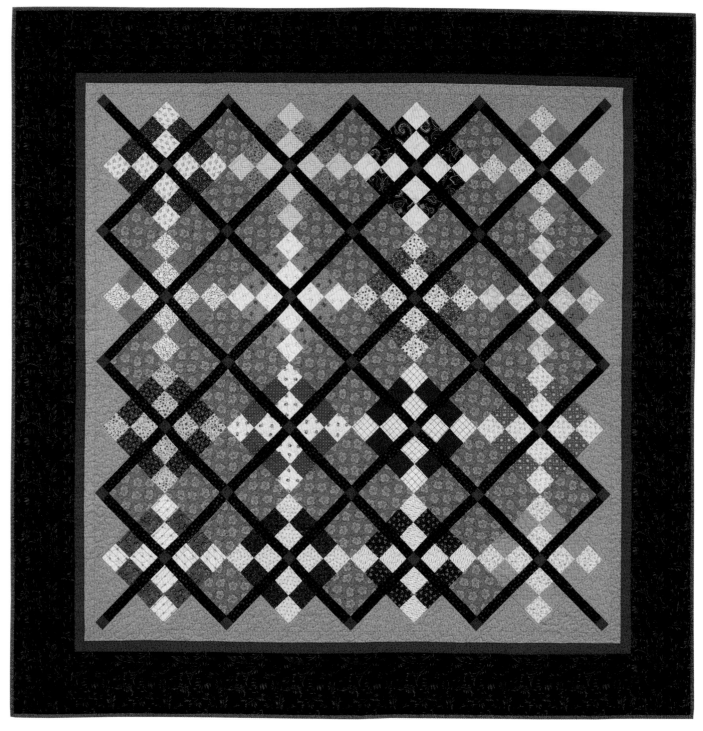

LATTICE MAKE A QUILT
Made by Lynn Roddy Brown.
Finished quilt: 70" x 70" • Finished block: 9" x 9" • Number of blocks: 16 (64 four-patch units)

LATTICE MAKE A QUILT

This quilt includes both a diagonal and a horizontal grid pattern. The two grids result from careful value placement. Choose very light fabrics along with a medium fabric for the four-patch units and a very dark fabric for what appears to be lattice forming the diagonal grid. Red is a strong color that works well as the accent.

MATERIALS

All yardages are based on 42"-wide fabric unless otherwise noted.

2¼ yards of black-and-gray floral for borders

⅞ yard of gray floral for alternate blocks

⅞ yard of light gray tone-on-tone fabric for setting triangles and inner border

⅞ yard of black-and-gray polka-dot fabric for lattice

½ yard of red fabric for cornerstones and inner border

16 assorted medium fabric strips, 2½" x 21", for four-patch units

16 assorted light fabric strips, 2½" x 21", for four-patch units

⅔ yard of medium gray fabric for binding

4¾ yards of fabric for backing

78" x 78" piece of batting

CUTTING

All measurements include ¼"-wide seam allowances.

From the black-and-gray polka-dot fabric, cut:
5 strips, 4½" x 42", crosscut into 128 rectangles, 1½" x 4½"

From the red fabric, cut:
8 strips, 1½" x 42"; crosscut 2 of the strips into 41 squares, 1½" x 1½".

From the gray floral cut:
6 strips, 4½" x 42"; crosscut into 48 squares, 4½" x 4½"

From the light gray tone-on-tone fabric cut:
2 strips, 9" x 42"; crosscut into 8 squares, 9" x 9". Cut each square diagonally twice to yield 32 setting triangles.
4 rectangles, 1½" x 2"
6 strips, 1½" x 42"

From the black-and-gray floral, cut:
2 strips, 7" x 64", from the *lengthwise* grain
2 strips, 7" x 74" from the *lengthwise* grain

From the medium gray fabric, cut:
8 strips, 2½" x 42"

MAKING BLOCKS WITH FOUR-PATCH UNITS

1. Sew a polka-dot rectangle to each side of a red square; press toward the polka-dot fabric. Make 16.

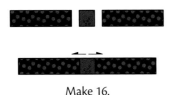

Make 16.

2. To make four-patch units, sew a light 2½" x 21" strip to a medium 2½" x 21" strip along the long sides; press toward the medium fabric. Cut the strip set into eight 2½" segments.

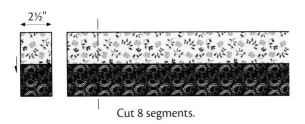

2½"

Cut 8 segments.

3. Place two segments right sides together with seams butting. Use straight pins to secure the seams. Sew the pair together as shown. Press the seam allowances open. Make four four-patch units.

Make 4.

4. Arrange the four-patch units, a pieced unit from step 1, and two polka-dot rectangles as shown. Join four-patch units to each side of the polka-dot lattice strips, making certain the four-patch units are in the correct position. Press the seam allowances toward the lattice. Join the rows together, carefully matching the seams. Press the seam allowances toward the lattice.

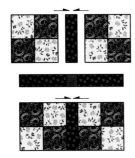

5. Repeat steps 2–4 to make a total of 16 blocks.

MAKING ALTERNATE BLOCKS

1. Join a polka-dot rectangle to each side of a red square. Press toward the red square. Make 9.

2. Arrange four gray floral squares, a pieced unit from step 1, and two polka-dot rectangles as shown. Join the gray floral squares to the polka-dot sashing strip. Press the seam allowances toward the gray floral. Join the rows together, carefully matching the seams. Press the seam allowances toward the gray floral.

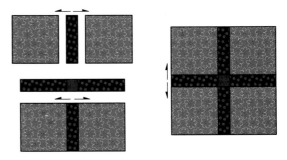

3. Repeat step 2 to make a total of nine alternate blocks.

MAKING SETTING TRIANGLES

1. To make the side setting triangles, sew a polka-dot rectangle to one side of a gray floral square. Press the seam allowance toward the floral.

2. Sew a red square to the end of a polka-dot rectangle; press toward the red square. Sew the pieced sashing strip to an adjacent side of the unit from step 1. Press the seam allowance toward the gray floral.

3. Align a gray tone-on-tone setting triangle with the unit from step 2 so that the right angle corner of the triangle aligns with the polka-dot corner. Starting at the corner, sew the seam that runs along the sashing edge. Press the seam allowance toward the setting triangle and trim the point as shown.

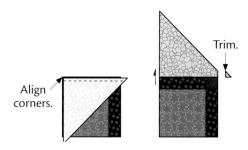

4. Add a second setting triangle, aligning the right-angle corner of the triangle with the remaining polka-dot corner. Starting at the corner, sew the seam that runs along the sashing edge; press toward the setting triangle.

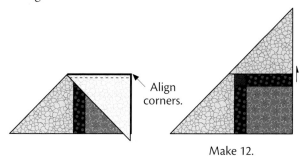

Make 12.

5. Repeat steps 1–4 to complete a total of 12 side setting triangles.

6. To make the corner setting triangles, sew a red square to the end of a polka-dot rectangle. Add a gray tone-on-tone rectangle to the opposite side of the red square. Press both seam allowances toward the polka-dot fabric. Make four.

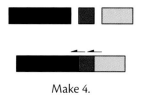

Make 4.

7. Align the right-angle corner of a gray tone-on-tone triangle with the polka-dot end of the sashing piece. Starting at the corner, sew the seam and press the seam allowance toward the triangle. Add a second triangle to the opposite side. Press the seam allowance

toward the triangle. Align a square ruler with the triangle edges and trim the rectangle to a point as shown. Make four corner triangles.

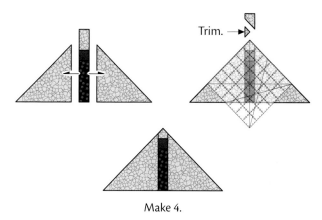

Make 4.

ASSEMBLING THE QUILT TOP

1. Working on a design wall and referring to the quilt diagram, arrange the Four Patch blocks and the alternate blocks in a diagonal set. Move the blocks around until you are happy with the arrangement. Add the pieced side and corner setting triangles to the design wall.

2. Join the blocks and side triangles into rows. Press the seam allowances toward the alternate blocks and setting triangles.

3. Join the diagonal rows. Press the seam allowances open. Add the corner triangles and press the seam allowances toward the corner triangles.

4. Note that the red squares of the setting triangles extend farther from the quilt edge than the Four Patch blocks. The quilt needs to be trimmed ¼" out from the red squares. Referring to "Diagonal Sets" on page 21, trim the quilt on all four sides leaving a ¼" seam allowance beyond the red squares.

5. Cut each of two 1½" x 42" gray tone-on-tone strips into two equal lengths. Using a diagonal seam, join each of the segments to the remaining four 42" border strips. Referring to "Borders with Butted Corners" on page 21, add the side borders; press the seam allowances outward. Add the top and bottom borders, and press the seam allowances outward.

6. Repeat step 5 using the six red strips. Press the seam allowances outward.

7. Piece and add the black-and-gray floral outer borders in the same manner. Press all the seam allowances outward.

FINISHING THE QUILT

1. Cut the backing fabric across the grain, into two equal pieces. Remove the selvages. Sew these pieces together along the lengthwise grain to create the back. Press the seam allowance open. The seam can run vertically or horizontally.

2. Prepare the quilt for quilting, referring to "Layering and Basting" on page 23.

3. Use the medium gray 2½" strips to bind the quilt, referring to "Binding" on page 24.

4. Make and attach a label to your quilt.

FOUR PATCH BLOCKS FOR TRADES

Finished size: 4" x 4" • Yield: 28

From one light fabric, cut:
4 strips, 2½" x 42"

From one medium to dark fabric, cut:
4 strips, 2½" x 42"

1. Sew a light strip to a medium to dark strip along their long sides; press toward the medium to dark fabric. Cut the strip set into 2½" segments.

2½"

Make 4 strip sets.
Cut 14 segments from each.

2. Pair the segments and place them right sides together with seams butting. Use straight pins to secure the seams. Sew and press the seam allowances open.

3. My group traded Four Patch blocks in groups of four identical blocks. Join four identical blocks with a pin or tack with thread.

ALTERNATE BLOCK LAYOUT

TURN OF EVENTS

Made by Lynn Roddy Brown.

Finished quilt: 30½" x 38½" • Finished block: 4" x 4"

I originally wanted to make a medallion quilt using four-patch units in the center. I sorted through my bag of four-patch units and chose the ones that didn't have a strong contrast in value. From those I selected the ones I felt went well together. Then I had a problem. I couldn't seem to find anything I wanted to use to surround the center. I finally decided to just make a small doll-sized quilt—something I rarely do. This is an example of keeping an open mind!

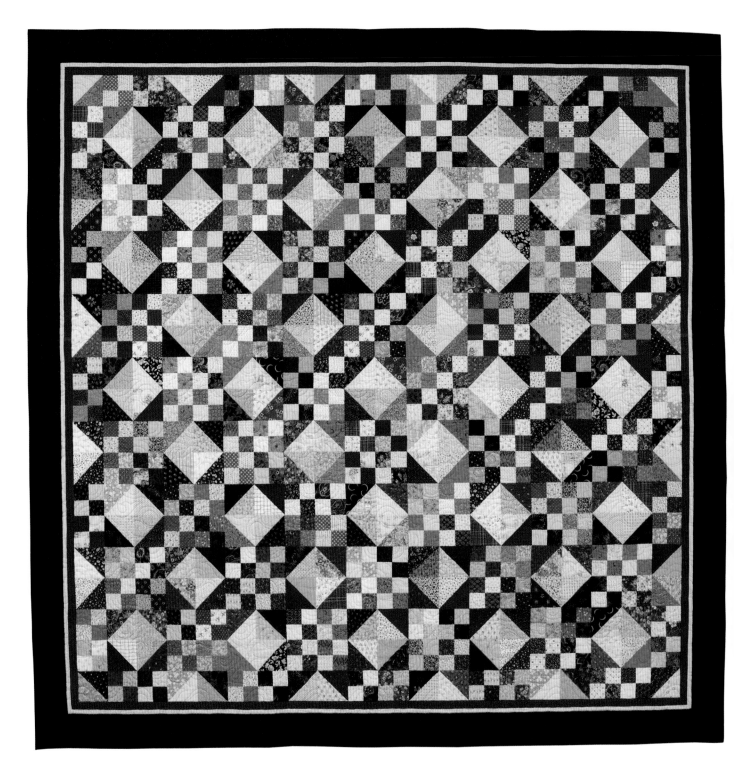

MONTANA SCRAPPY
Made by Judy Fogelsong. Machine quilted by Sharon Dixon.
Finished quilt: 92" x 92" • Finished block: 8" x 8"
Number of half-square-triangle units: 200 • Number of four-patch units: 200

MONTANA SCRAPPY

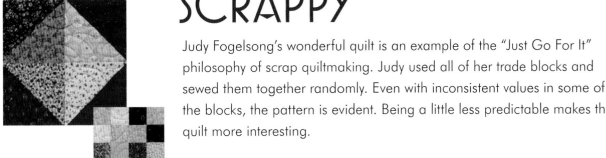

Judy Fogelsong's wonderful quilt is an example of the "Just Go For It" philosophy of scrap quiltmaking. Judy used all of her trade blocks and sewed them together randomly. Even with inconsistent values in some of the blocks, the pattern is evident. Being a little less predictable makes the quilt more interesting.

MATERIALS

All yardages are based on 42"-wide fabric unless otherwise noted.

4⅔ yards *total* of medium/dark scraps for half-square-triangle and four-patch units

4⅔ yards *total* of light scraps for half-square-triangle and four-patch units

2½ yards of navy print for outer border and binding

⅝ yard of red print for inner border

½ yard cream print for middle border

9 yards of fabric for backing

100" x 100" piece of batting

CUTTING

All measurements include ¼"-wide seam allowances.

From the medium/dark scraps, cut:
100 squares, 5¼" x 5¼"
200 rectangles, 2½" x 5½"

From the light scraps, cut:
100 squares, 5¼" x 5¼"
200 rectangles, 2½" x 5½"

From the red print, cut:
12 strips, 1½" x 42"

From the cream print, cut:
12 strips, 1" x 42"

From the navy print, cut:
12 strips, 4¾" x 42"
10 strips, 2½" x 42"

MAKING THE BLOCKS

For this quilt, you'll need 50 of block A and 50 of Block B. Each block is made from two four-patch units and two half-square-triangle units. The difference between the blocks is determined by the placement of the values in the four-patch units.

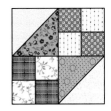   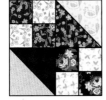

Block A   Block B

Making the Half-Square-Triangle Units

Select a light and a medium/dark square. Refer to "Half-Square-Triangle Units" on page 18 to make two identical units from the pair of squares. Press the seam allowances toward the medium/dark fabric and trim completed units to 4½" square. Make 200 half-square-triangle units.

Make 200.

Making the Four-Patch Units

1. Sew a light rectangle to a medium/dark rectangle along their long sides. Press toward the medium/dark fabric. Cut the strip set into two 2½" segments.

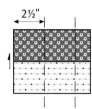

2. Place the segments from step 1 right sides together with seams butting. Use a straight pin to secure the seam; sew together and press the seam allowance open. Make 200 four-patch units.

Make 200.

Making Block A

1. Select two different half-square-triangle units and two different four-patch units. Arrange the units as shown. Make certain the light fabric of the four-patch units is positioned correctly.

2. Sew the pieces of each block together in rows and press the seam allowances toward the four-patch units. Sew the rows together and press the seam allowances open. Make 50 blocks.

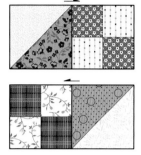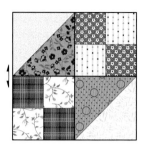

Block A.
Make 50.

Making Block B

1. Select two different half-square-triangle units and two different four-patch units. Arrange the units as shown. Make certain the dark fabric of the four-patch units is positioned correctly.

2. Sew the pieces of each block together in rows and press the seam allowances toward the four-patch units. Sew the rows together and press the seam allowances open. Make 50 blocks.

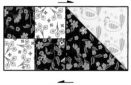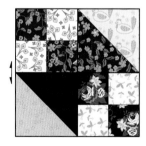

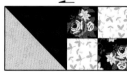

Block B.
Make 50.

ASSEMBLING THE QUILT TOP

1. Arrange the blocks in 10 horizontal rows of 10 blocks each, referring to the quilt diagram below. The A and B blocks alternate from row to row, with the top row beginning with an A block and ending with a B block.

2. Join the blocks in rows. Press the seam allowances open.

3. Join the rows. Press the seam allowances open.

4. To add mitered borders, it will be easier to sew the three borders for each side together first and then add them as a unit. Sew three red strips together end to end using a diagonal seam. Press the seam allowances open. Make four. Repeat using the cream strips and the navy 4¾" strips.

5. Sew a red inner-border strip to a cream inner-border strip. Press the seam allowances open. Sew this unit to a navy border strip, making certain that the cream border is in the middle. Press the seam allowances open. Repeat to make four border units.

6. Add the borders, referring to "Borders with Mitered Corners" on page 22.

FINISHING THE QUILT

1. Cut the backing fabric across the grain into three equal pieces. Remove the selvages. Sew these pieces together along the lengthwise grain to create the quilt back. Press the seam allowances open. The seams can run vertically or horizontally.

2. Refer to "Layering and Basting" on page 23; hand or machine quilt as desired.

3. Use the navy 2½"-strips to bind the quilt, referring to "Binding" on page 24.

4. Make and attach a label to your quilt.

ALTERNATE BLOCK LAYOUT

JACOB'S LADDER

Made by Fran Urquhart. Machine quilted by Sharon Dixon.
Finished quilt: 94½" x 106½" • Finished block: 12" x 12"

Fran Urquhart used all of her blocks from the trade to make this scrappy version of Jacob's Ladder. She went through her stash and found a blue that she felt was perfect for the border, but she only had one yard. This explains the red-and-blue four-patch units and the width of the border. Not having enough fabric should be thought of as an opportunity to be creative.

ALTERNATE BLOCK LAYOUT

SUNSHINE ON MY SHOULDERS

Made by Fran Urquhart. Machine quilted by Sharon Dixon.
Finished quilt: 104½" x 104½" • Finished block: 16" x 16"

When we traded half-square-triangle units and four-patch units in blues and yellows, Fran Urquhart used the Sunny Lane block to make this magnificent quilt. Notice how she extended the block pattern into the borders.

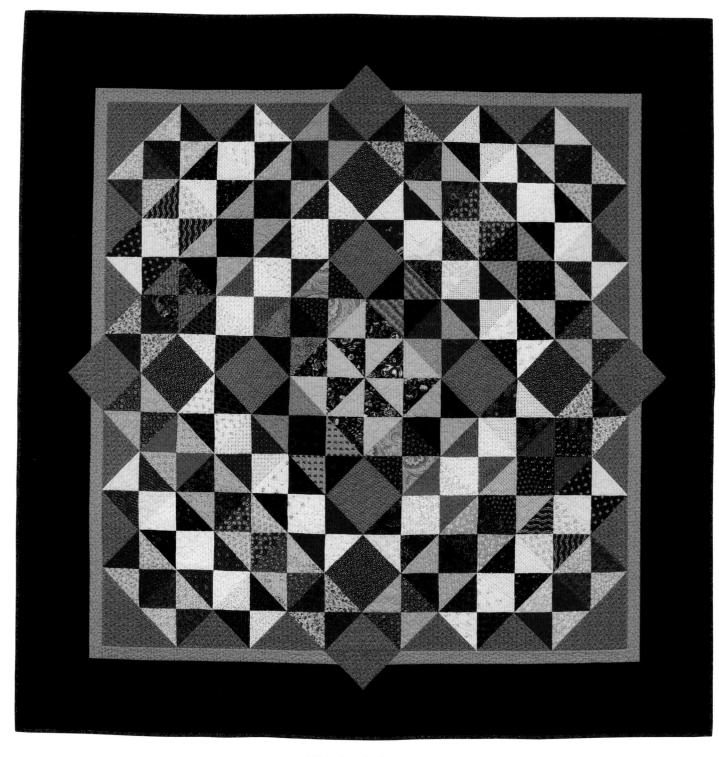

ORDER OUT OF CHAOS
Made by Lynn Roddy Brown. Blocks provided by Rita Carter.
Finished quilt: 79" x 79" • Finished block: 6" x 6" • Number of blocks: 76

HOURGLASS BLOCKS

ORDER OUT OF CHAOS

This set of traded Hourglass blocks had inconsistent values, which often makes it difficult to form an overall pattern. I first sorted the blocks into two groups; blocks with one very light fabric, and blocks with only medium to dark. I found four identical blocks, which became the center. I found eight blocks that combined medium brown with darker fabrics to surround the four center blocks. Blocks using one very light fabric came next, followed by a row of medium/dark blocks. As I worked outward, I made a few additional blocks in the values needed.

MATERIALS

All yardages are based on 42"-wide fabric unless otherwise noted.

2½ yards black print for outer border

1⅜ yards *total* of medium dark scraps for Hourglass blocks

1⅛ yards of medium brown print for setting triangles

1 yard *total* of medium scraps for Hourglass blocks

1 yard *total* of light scraps for Hourglass blocks

⅝ yard of medium pink tone-on-tone fabric for inner border

⅓ yard *total* of medium light scraps for Hourglass blocks

1 fat quarter of medium brown fabric for plain blocks

1 fat quarter medium/dark small-scale floral for plain blocks

1 square, 7½" x 7½", *each* of 4 assorted medium brown prints for Hourglass blocks

1 square, 7½" x 7½", *each* of 4 assorted black, burgundy, or dark brown squares for Hourglass blocks

2 squares, 7½" x 7½", of light pink fabric for center Hourglass blocks

2 squares, 7½" x 7½", of black floral for center Hourglass blocks

¾ yard of medium brown fabric for binding

7½ yards of fabric for backing*

87" x 87" piece of batting

*Consider piecing extra fabric strips to make an 87" length. Sew this pieced strip crosswise into (seam for) the backing. Using this method, you would need 5⅓ yards of backing fabric.

CUTTING

All measurements include ¼"-wide seam allowances.

From the medium dark scraps, cut:
28 squares, 7½" x 7½"

From the light scraps, cut:
16 squares, 7½" x 7½"

From the medium scraps, cut:
16 squares, 7½" x 7½"

From the medium light scraps, cut:
4 squares, 7½" x 7½"

From the fat quarter of medium brown fabric, cut:
4 squares, 6½" x 6½"

From the fat quarter of medium/dark small-scale floral, cut:
4 squares, 6½" x 6½"

From the medium brown print, cut:
3 strips, 10½" x 42"; crosscut into 7 squares, 10½" x 10½"; cut 5 squares twice diagonally to yield 20 side triangles; cut 2 squares once diagonally to yield 4 corner triangles.

2 squares, 7¼" x 7¼"; cut once diagonally to yield 4 border triangles.

From the medium pink tone-on-tone fabric, cut:
8 strips, 2" x 42"

From the black print, cut:
2 strips, 8½" x 67" from the *lengthwise* grain
2 strips, 8½" x 83" from the *lengthwise* grain

From the medium brown fabric, cut:
9 strips, 2½" x 42"

MAKING HOURGLASS BLOCKS

For each set of two blocks you will need two 7½" squares.

1. Refer to "Half-Square-Triangle Units" on page 18. Pair a light square with a medium dark square. Cut the paired fabrics diagonally to form two triangles. Sew the diagonal seams of the triangle pairs; press toward the medium dark fabric to make two identical half-square-triangle units. Do not trim.

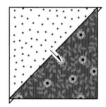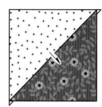

2. Place the two half-square-triangle units right sides together, aligning the edges and butting the opposing seams. Check to make certain the light sides of the units are on opposite sides of the nested seam. Cut the nested pair diagonally across the seam. Before moving the units from the mat, place one pin in each unit to hold them together. Sew the seam and press the seam allowances open.

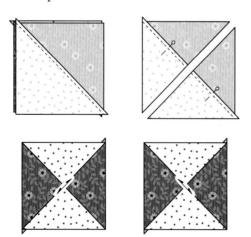

3. Trim the hourglass units to 6½" square by placing the 45° diagonal line of a small square ruler along one of the seam lines. Position the 3¼" mark of the ruler on the unit center and trim the two adjacent sides. Rotate the unit so the trimmed edges are under the ruler on the 6½" mark. Trim the remaining sides.

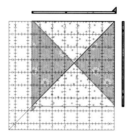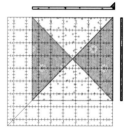

Trim units 6½" square.

4. Repeat steps 1–3 using the 7½" squares of all values. Pair the remaining 15 light and medium dark squares to make 30 blocks (32 total). Pair 12 medium with medium dark to make 24 blocks. Pair four medium light with medium to make 8 blocks. Pair four medium brown with the darker black, burgundy, or dark brown to make 8 blocks. Pair the two pink squares with the black floral squares to make four blocks.

Light and medium dark. Make 32.　　Medium and medium dark. Make 24.　　Medium light and medium. Make 8.

Medium brown and dark. Make 8.　　Pink and black floral. Make 4.

ASSEMBLING THE QUILT TOP

1. Using a design wall and referring to the quilt diagram, start in the center and arrange the Hourglass blocks, plain blocks, and the side setting triangles into diagonal rows.

2. Sew the blocks and side setting triangles into diagonal rows, referring to "Diagonal Sets" on page 21. Press the seam allowances open.

3. Join the rows and press the seam allowances open. Add the corner triangles. Press the seam allowances outward. Trim the quilt on all four sides, leaving a ¼" seam allowance.

4. Press under ¼" on the two short sides of the four brown print 7¼" triangles for the border.

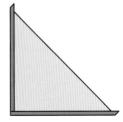

5. Position a border triangle, right sides together, with the setting triangle that is in the center of each side. Align the pressed-under edges of the border triangles with the seams of the setting triangles and pin. The border triangles are oversized and will extend beyond the edge of the quilt. Trim the border triangles even with the edge of the quilt; they will be joined to the top when the pink tone-on-tone inner borders are added.

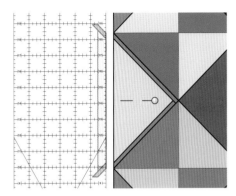

6. For each of the four pink inner borders sew two 2" strips end to end using a diagonal seam. Press the seam allowances open.

7. Referring to "Borders with Butted Corners" on page 21, add the pink side borders and then the top and bottom. The border triangles will be sewn into the seam allowance. Press the seam allowance toward the border, but leave the triangles pinned to the quilt top until the outer borders are added.

8. Add the black outer side borders and then the top and bottom, pressing the seam allowance toward the borders.

9. Remove pins and press the border triangles over the inner and outer borders. Pin in place and topstitch by machine or sew by hand.

FINISHING THE QUILT

1. Cut the backing fabric across the grain into three equal pieces. Remove the selvages. Sew these pieces together along the lengthwise grain to create the quilt back. Press the seam allowances open. The seam allowances can run vertically or horizontally.

2. Refer to "Layering and Basting" on page 23; hand or machine quilt as desired.

3. Use the medium brown 2½" strips to bind the quilt, referring to "Binding" on page 24.

4. Make and attach a label to your quilt.

HOURGLASS BLOCKS FOR TRADES

Finished size: 6" x 6" • Yield: 10

From one light fabric, cut:
1 strip, 7½" x 42"; crosscut into 5 squares, 7½" x 7½"

From one medium to dark fabric, cut:
1 strip, 7½" x 42"; crosscut into 5 squares, 7½" x 7½"

Pair each light square with a medium to dark square and refer to steps 1–3 of "Making Hourglass Blocks" on page 46.

COUNTRY COUSINS

Denise Goodman is another member of our group who uses the "Just Go For It" approach to quiltmaking. She combined blocks from the Hourglass trade with those from the Nine Patch trade, and then used a wonderful border print that gives the impression of an inner border. I find this quilt very intriguing. As you look at it, you will see large stars appear and disappear over the surface of the quilt.

MATERIALS

All yardages are based on 42"-wide fabric unless otherwise noted.

2⅔ yards of floral border print with four repeats

2¼ yards *total* of medium to dark scraps for Hourglass and Nine Patch blocks

2¼ yards *total* of light to medium/light scraps for Hourglass and Nine Patch blocks

1 yard of cream print for setting triangles

⅔ yard of medium brown print for binding

5½ yards of fabric for backing

73" x 90" piece of batting

CUTTING

All measurements include ¼"-wide seam allowances.

From the medium to dark scraps, cut:

24 squares, 7½" x 7½"

90 squares, 2½" x 2½", in 18 matching sets of 5

68 squares, 2½" x 2½", in 17 matching sets of 4

From the light to medium/light scraps, cut:

24 squares, 7½" x 7½" squares

72 squares, 2½" x 2½", in 18 matching sets of 4

85 squares, 2½" x 2½", in 17 matching sets of 5

From the cream print, cut:

2 strips, 11" x 42"; crosscut into 6 squares, 11" x 11". Cut each square twice diagonally to yield 24 side triangles.

2 squares, 6 ½" x 6 ½". Cut each square once diagonally to yield 4 corner triangles.

From the floral border print*, cut:

4 strips, 7" x 88" on the *lengthwise* grain

From the medium brown print, cut:

8 strips, 2½" x 42"

*Depending on your print, you may need to cut your strips slightly wider or narrower.

COUNTRY COUSINS
Made by Denise Goodman. Machine quilted by Linda Hillman.
Finished quilt: 64½" x 81½" • Finished block: 6" x 6"
Number of Hourglass blocks: 48 • Number of Nine Patch blocks: 18 X and 17 O

MAKING HOURGLASS BLOCKS

Referring to "Making Hourglass Blocks" on page 46, pair light 7½" squares with medium to dark squares to make 48 blocks. You might consider making some blocks using a medium with a dark. The values in the quilt shown aren't consistent.

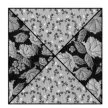

Make 48.

MAKING NINE PATCH BLOCKS

You will need to make Nine Patch blocks with opposite placement of the dark and light values. The blocks with five dark squares are X blocks, and those with four dark squares are O blocks. You need 18 X blocks and 17 O blocks.

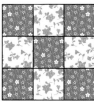

Block X   Block O

1. Select five matching medium to dark 2½"squares and four matching light 2½" squares. Arrange the squares in rows as shown making certain the values are in the correct positions. Sew the squares together in rows and press the seam allowances toward the medium to dark squares. Pin and sew the top and bottom units to the center unit, matching seams. Press the seam allowances open. Make a total of 18 blocks.

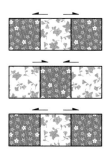

Make 18.

2. Select five matching light 2½" squares and four matching medium to dark 2½" squares. Arrange the squares in rows as shown making certain the values are in the correct positions. Sew the squares together in rows and press the seam allowances toward the medium to dark squares. Pin and sew the top and bottom units to the center unit, matching seams. Press the seam allowances open. Make a total of 17 blocks.

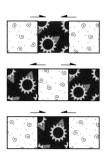

Make 17.

ASSEMBLING THE QUILT TOP

1. Referring to the quilt diagram on page 52, arrange the Hour-glass and Nine Patch blocks in diagonal rows on a design wall. Note that the position of the darks in the Hourglass blocks alternates from row to row, and the X and O Nine Patch blocks alternate. Also notice that the X blocks are surrounded with the lighter values of the Hourglass blocks and the O blocks are surrounded by the darker values. Inconsistent values in the blocks may blur the pattern.

2. Add the side triangles to the layout. Referring to "Diagonal Sets" on page 21, join the blocks and side triangles in diagonal rows. Press the seam allowances open. Join the rows and press the seam allowances open. Add the corner triangles; press the seam allowances outward.

3. Trim the quilt on all four sides, leaving a ¼" seam allowance.

4. Add the floral borders referring to "Borders with Mitered Corners" on page 22.

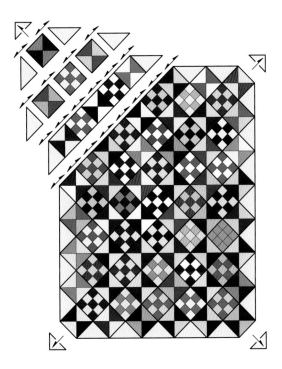

FINISHING THE QUILT

1. Cut the backing fabric across the grain into two equal pieces. Remove the selvages. Sew the pieces together along the lengthwise grain to create the quilt back. Press the seam allowance open. The seam will run vertically on the quilt.

2. Refer to "Layering and Basting" on page 23; hand or machine quilt as desired.

3. Use the medium brown 2½" strips to bind the quilt, referring to "Binding" on page 24.

4. Make and attach a label to your quilt.

NINE PATCH BLOCKS FOR TRADES

Finished size: 6" x 6"
Yield: 5 X blocks and 5 O blocks

From one medium to dark fabric, cut:
3 strips, 2½" x 42"

From one light fabric, cut:
3 strips, 2½" x 42"

1. Make two strip sets as shown. Press the seam allowances toward the medium to dark. Cut each strip set into 15 segments, 2½" wide.

Cut 15 segments from each.

2. Arrange the segments into five X blocks and five O blocks. Pin and sew the segments together, matching seams. Press the seam allowances open.

Make 5.

Make 5.

When my group did this trade, the X Nine Patch blocks were traded separately from the O Nine Patch blocks. Members could make either type or both.

ALTERNATE BLOCK LAYOUT

HOURGLASS: SECOND CHANCE

Made by Lynn Roddy Brown.
Finished quilt: 68" x 85" • Finished block: 6" x 6"

In this quilt I used most of the Hourglass blocks that were left after making "Order Out of Chaos" on page 45. I've found that if blocks don't seem to go well together, separating them can be a solution. My quilt is very similar to Denise's "Country Cousins." I replaced the Nine Patch blocks with setting blocks in light and medium/dark values. I'm not a "Just Go For It" quilter. I worked very hard to achieve consistent values. This makes the overall pattern of my quilt much clearer, but I think Denise's quilt is more interesting.

BARN RAISING
Made by Lynn Roddy Brown. Blocks provided by Denise Goodman.
Finished quilt: 67½" x 67½" • Finished block: 6" x 6" • Number of blocks: 64

BARN RAISING

Barn Raising is the name traditionally given to a specific Log Cabin setting. Like the Log Cabin block, the Split Nine Patch block has a strong diagonal line created by value. It is the diagonal line that allows for many setting possibilities.

For the overall pattern to be seen across the surface of this quilt, the values in the blocks must be consistent. The lights must be within the same value range and lighter than any of the medium to dark fabrics. When making this quilt, all the fabrics to be used should be sorted into a group of lights and a group of medium to darks. If a fabric doesn't seem to fit into either group, I wouldn't use it.

MATERIALS

All yardages are based on 42"-wide fabric unless otherwise noted.

2¼ yards of gray print for outer border

2 yards *total* of medium to dark scraps for blocks

1⅝ yards *total* of light scraps for blocks

⅔ yard of beige striped fabric for inner border

⅔ yard of dark gray fabric for binding

4½ yards of fabric for backing

76" x 76" piece of batting

CUTTING

All measurements include ¼"-wide seam allowances.

From the medium to dark scraps, cut:
256 squares, 2½" x 2½"
64 squares, 3¼" x 3¼"

From the light scraps, cut:
192 squares, 2½" x 2½"
64 squares, 3¼" x 3¼"

From the beige striped fabric, cut:
8 strips, 2½" x 42"

From the gray print, cut:
2 strips, 8" x 57" from the *lengthwise* grain
2 strips, 8" x 72" from the *lengthwise* grain

From the dark gray fabric, cut:
8 strips, 2½" x 42"

MAKING THE BLOCKS

1. Referring to "Half-Square-Triangle Units" on page 18, pair a light 3¼" square with a medium to dark 3¼" square. Make 2 identical half-square-triangle units from each pair, for a total of 128. Press the seam allowances toward the medium to dark fabric and trim the units to 2½" square.

2. For each block you will need three different light 2½" squares, four different medium to dark 2 ½" squares and two different half-square-triangle units. Lay out the squares as shown.

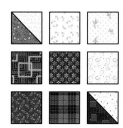

3. Sew the pieces together in rows. Press the seam allowances in the direction of the arrows in the diagram. Join the rows and press the seam allowances open. Make 64 blocks.

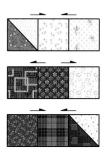 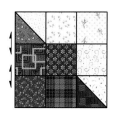

Make 64.

ASSEMBLING THE QUILT TOP

1. Working on your design wall, arrange the blocks in eight horizontal rows of eight blocks each. Referring to the quilt diagram, rotate the blocks to create the design.

2. Join the blocks into rows. Press the seam allowances open. Join the rows and press the seam allowances open.

3. Sew the beige striped 2½" strips together in pairs end to end using a straight seam and matching the stripe. Press the seam allowances open.

4. Referring to "Borders with Butted Corners" on page 21, add the striped borders to the sides. Press the seam allowances toward the borders. Add the borders to the top and bottom; press.

5. Add the gray 8" x 57" strips to the sides. Press the seam allowances toward the borders. Add the gray 8" x 72" strips to the top and bottom; press.

FINISHING THE QUILT

1. Cut the backing fabric across the grain into two equal pieces. Remove the selvages. Sew these pieces together along the lengthwise grain to create the quilt back. Press the seam allowance open. The seam can run vertically or horizontally.

2. Refer to "Layering and Basting" on page 23; hand or machine quilt as desired.

3. Use the dark gray 2½" strips to bind the quilt, referring to "Binding" on page 24.

4. Make and attach a label to your quilt.

SPLIT NINE PATCH BLOCKS FOR TRADES

Finished size: 6" x 6" • Yield: 8

From 5 different light prints, cut:
1 strip *each of 3 different prints*, 2½" x 21"
1 square *each of 2 different prints*, 6" x 6"

From 6 different medium to dark prints, cut:
1 strip *each of 4 different prints*, 2½" x 21"
1 square *each of 2 different prints*, 6" x 6"

1. Make three strip sets as shown. Cut each strip set into eight 2½"-wide segments.

2. Referring to "Half-Square-Triangle Units" on page 18, pair the light and medium to dark squares to make 8 identical units from each pair. Press the seam allowances toward the medium to dark fabric and trim completed units to 2½" x 2½".

3. Arrange the units made in steps 1 and 2 as shown. Sew the pieces together in vertical rows. Press the seam allowances as shown. Join the rows and press the seam allowances open. Make 8 identical blocks.

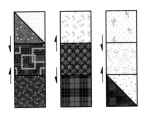

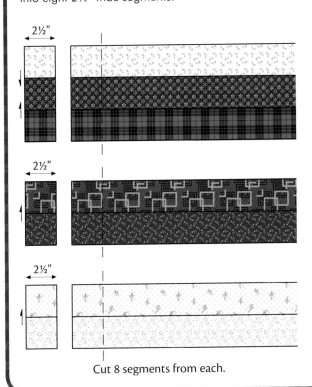

Cut 8 segments from each.

Make 8.

EVERY WHICH WAY
Made by Janice Thompson and Lynn Roddy Brown.
Finished quilt: 55½" x 67½" • Finished block: 6" x 6" • Number of blocks: 63

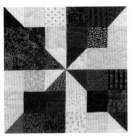

EVERY WHICH WAY

This quilt uses an uneven setting of seven blocks across and nine down (7 x 9), which helps keep the viewer's eye moving. Notice that the four blocks in the upper-left corner form a pinwheel while the four blocks in the upper-right corner form a different pattern. If the blocks had been set 6 x 8 or 8 x 10, the same block pattern would be seen in all four corners.

MATERIALS

All yardages are based on 42"-wide fabric unless otherwise noted.

2½ yards of red-and-gold print for border and binding

2 yards *total* of medium to dark scraps for blocks

1⅝ yards *total* of light scraps for blocks

½ yard of gold print for inner border

4 yards of fabric for backing

64" x 76" piece of batting

CUTTING

All measurements include ¼"-wide seam allowances.

From the medium to dark scraps, cut:

252 squares, 2½" x 2½"

63 squares, 3¼" x 3¼"

From the light scraps, cut:

189 squares, 2½" x 2½"

63 squares, 3¼" x 3¼"

From the gold print, cut:

8 strips, 1½" x 42"

From the red-and-gold print, cut:

4 strips, 6" x 61" from the *lengthwise* grain

7 strips, 2½" x 42"

MAKING THE BLOCKS

Refer to "Making the Blocks" on page 55. Make 126 half-square-triangle units and 63 Split Nine Patch blocks.

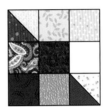

Make 63.

ASSEMBLING THE QUILT TOP

1. Working on a design wall, arrange the blocks in nine horizontal rows of seven blocks each. Referring to the quilt diagram on page 60 and the photo on page 58, rotate the blocks as shown.

2. Join the blocks into rows; press the seam allowances open. Join the rows and press the seam allowances open.

3. Sew the gold 1½" inner-border strips together in pairs end to end using a diagonal seam. Press the seam allowances open.

4. Referring to "Borders with Butted Corners" on page 21, add the side inner borders. Press the seam allowances toward the borders. Add the top and bottom inner borders and press.

5. Add the red-and-gold outer borders to the sides using two of the 6" x 61" strips.; press the seam allowances toward the borders. Add the red-and-gold 6" x 61" strips to the top and bottom; press.

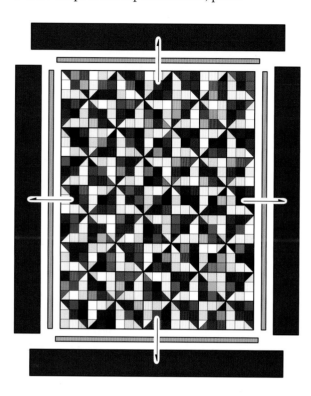

FINISHING THE QUILT

1. Cut the backing fabric across the grain into two equal pieces. Remove the selvages. Sew these pieces together along the lengthwise grain to create the quilt back. Press the seam allowance open. The seam will run horizontally on the quilt.

2. Refer to "Layering and Basting" on page 23; hand or machine quilt as desired.

3. Use the red-and-gold 2½"-strips to bind the quilt, referring to "Binding" on page 24.

4. Make and attach a label to your quilt.

ALTERNATE BLOCK LAYOUT

SQUARE DANCE

Made by Barbara Reynolds.

Finished quilt: 100" x 125" • Finished block: 6" x 6"

Barbara's quilt is a fabulous example of what can be done when a block has a diagonal line.

ZIGZAG
Made by Lynn Roddy Brown.
Finished quilt: 74" x 87" • Finished block: 9" x 9" • Number of blocks: 32

ZIGZAG

This trade was done using Civil War reproduction fabrics. The lighter backgrounds are warm colors, many of which appear tea dyed. If the value placement in this block is altered, different patterns appear. Many antique quilts include blocks made with different value placement. Most of my group wanted consistent values for the trade. Those of us who wanted an added challenge did a side trade of blocks with varying value placement. In my quilt there are three blocks that appear to be entirely different and several with the values reversed. Darra Duffy Williamson, in her book *Sensational Scrap Quilts,* says she changes the value placement in one out of four blocks.

MATERIALS

All yardages are based on 42"-wide fabric unless otherwise noted.

4¾ yards of brown-and-orange print for setting triangles and outer border

⅔ yard of beige striped fabric for inner border

¼ yard* *each of* 32 light fabrics for Churn Dash blocks (2⅜ yards *total* of light scraps)

¼ yard* *each of* 32 medium to dark prints for Churn Dash blocks (2 yards *total* of medium to dark scraps)

¾ yard of orange tone-on-tone fabric for binding

5⅞ yards of fabric for backing

82" x 95" piece of batting

*You can use 32 fat eighths if you prefer. A standard ⅛-yard piece may be too narrow after prewashing.

CUTTING

All measurements include ¼"-wide seam allowances. The cutting instructions are written to make 32 A blocks. See "Making the Churn Dash Blocks" at right if you want to vary the value placement.

From *each* of the medium to dark prints, cut:

2 squares, 4¼" x 4¼" (64 total)

1 strip, 2" x 16" (32 total)

From *each* of the light fabrics, cut:

2 squares, 4¼" x 4¼" (64 total)

1 strip, 2" x 16" (32 total)

1 square, 3½" x 3½" (32 total)

From the beige striped fabric, cut:

8 strips, 2½" x 42"

From the brown-and-orange print, cut:

7 strips, 15" x 42"; crosscut into 14 squares, 15" x 15"; cut each square twice diagonally to yield 56 side triangles (2 are extra)

2 strips, 8½" x 42"; crosscut into 6 squares, 8½" x 8½"; cut each square once diagonally to yield 12 corner triangles

9 strips, 3½" x 42"

From the orange tone-on-tone fabric, cut:

9 strips, 2½" x 42"

MAKING THE CHURN DASH BLOCKS

The instructions are written for two fabrics in a block, with the lighter fabric being used for the background (block A). To reverse the value placement, cut the medium to dark pieces from light and the light pieces from medium to dark. Feel free to include additional fabrics as in blocks B and C shown below.

For each block A, you will need:

• 2 squares, 4¼" x 4¼", and 1 strip, 2" x 16" from one medium to dark fabric

• 2 squares, 4¼" x 4¼", 1 strip, 2" x 16", and 1 square 3½" x 3½" from one light fabric

A   B   C

1. Choose the two fabrics that you want for a block. Pair each light 4¼" square with a medium to dark 4¼" square. Refer to "Half-Square-Triangle Units" on page 18 to make two identical units (four total). Press the seam allowances toward the medium to dark fabric and trim completed units to 3½" square.

2. Sew together the light 2" x 16" strip and the medium to dark 2" x 16" strip along one long edge. Press the seam allowance toward the medium to dark fabric. Cut four 3½" segments as shown.

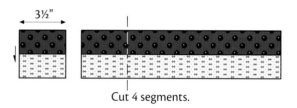

Cut 4 segments.

3. Arrange the half-square-triangle units from step 1, the strip segments from step 2, and the 3½" square as shown. Sew the units together in rows. Press seam allowances as indicated by arrows in the diagram. Sew the rows together carefully matching the seams. Press the final seam allowances open.

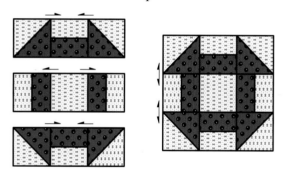

4. Repeat steps 1–3 to make a total of 32 Churn Dash blocks in a variety of fabrics. Alter value placement if desired.

ASSEMBLING THE QUILT TOP

1. Arrange the Churn Dash blocks, side triangles, and corner triangles into five vertical panels. Panels 1, 3, and 5 each have six blocks, 10 side triangles, and four corner triangles. Panels 2 and 4 each have seven blocks and 12 side triangles. Align the corners of the triangles with the corners of the blocks and sew together. Press the seam allowances toward the triangles.

2. Trim the points even with the edge of the blocks. Matching the seams of the units, join the units into panels. Add the corner triangles to panels 1, 3, and 5, and press the seam allowances outward.

Panels 1, 3, and 5

Panels 2 and 4

3. Referring to "Diagonal Sets" on page 21, trim the panels on the two long sides, leaving a ¼" seam allowance beyond the block points.

4. Join the panels and press the seam allowances open. Trim the top and bottom of the quilt top ¼" away from the tips of the Churn Dash blocks in panels 1, 3, and 5 and ¼" away from the center of the Churn Dash blocks in panels 2 and 4.

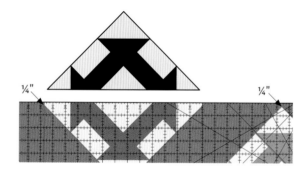

5. Sew pairs of beige striped 2½"-wide strips together end to end to make four inner-border strips, matching the stripes and using a straight seam.

6. Referring to "Borders with Butted Corners" on page 21, add the side borders. Press the seam allowance toward the borders. Add the top and bottom borders and press the seam allowances toward the borders.

7. Sew pairs of 3½"-wide brown-and-orange strips end to end using a diagonal seam to make four long border strips. Cut an additional brown and orange strip into two equal lengths. Sew the half strips to the ends of two of the borders using a diagonal seam. Press the seam allowances open. Add the longer strips to the sides and press toward the borders. Add the remaining strips to the top and bottom. Press the seam allowances toward the borders.

FINISHING THE QUILT

1. Cut the backing fabric across the grain into two equal pieces. Remove the selvages. Sew these pieces together along the lengthwise grain to create the quilt back. Press the seam allowance open. The seam will run vertically on the quilt.

2. Refer to "Layering and Basting" on page 23; hand or machine quilt as desired.

3. Use the orange tone-on-tone 2½" strips to bind the quilt, referring to "Binding" on page 24.

4. Make and attach a label to your quilt.

CHURN DASH BLOCKS FOR TRADES

Block size: 9" x 9" • Yield: 8

From one medium to dark fabric, cut:
3 strips, 2" x 42"
1 strip, 8" x 42"; crosscut into 4 squares, 8" x 8"

From one light fabric, cut:
3 strips, 2" x 42"
1 strip, 8" x 42"; crosscut into 4 squares, 8" x 8"
1 strip, 3½" x 42"; crosscut into 8 squares,
      3½" x 3½"

1. Pair each light 8" square with a medium to dark 8" square, referring to "Half-Square-Triangle Units" on page 18 to make 8 identical units from each pair. Press the seam allowances toward the medium to dark fabric and trim completed units to 3½" x 3½". Make a total of 32.

2. Sew each light 2" x 42" strip to a medium to dark strip along one long edge to make three strip sets. Press the seam allowances toward the medium to dark fabric. Cut 32 segments, 3½" wide.

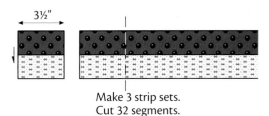

Make 3 strip sets.
Cut 32 segments.

3. Arrange the half-square-triangle units, the strip set segments, and the 3½" squares as shown. Sew the units together in rows. Press the seam allowances as indicated. Sew the rows together carefully matching the seams. Press the final seam allowances open. Make 8.

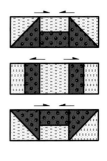
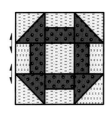

Make 8.

CHURNED-UP GEESE
Made by Elizabeth (Liz) Broussard.
Finished quilt: 87½" x 99½" • Finished block: 9" x 9" • Number of blocks: 56

CHURNED-UP GEESE

Liz Broussard's flying-geese sashing makes half of the Churn Dash blocks appear to be on point. When Liz was making her blocks for the trade, she also made flying-geese units in sets of four. After the trade when she had her blocks on the design wall, she paired sets of flying-geese units with Churn Dash blocks of similar color or value. If you look closely, you will notice a few Churn Dash blocks that have different value placements.

MATERIALS

All yardages are based on 42"-wide fabric unless otherwise noted.

3⅞ yards *total* of light scraps for sashing

3¼ yards *total* of medium to dark scraps for sashing

¼ yard *each of 56* light fabrics for Churn Dash blocks (or 4 ½ yards *total* of scraps)*

¼ yard *each of 56* medium to dark prints for Churn Dash blocks (or 3 ½ yards *total* of scraps*

⅞ yard of fabric for binding**

8¾ yards of fabric for backing

96" x 108" piece of batting

You can use 56 fat eighths if you prefer. A standard ⅛-yard piece may be too narrow after prewashing.
**The binding on the quilt shown is pieced from scraps. If you choose to make a scrappy binding, you will need a total length of 386".*

CUTTING

All measurements include ¼"-wide seam allowances.

From *each* of the 56 medium to dark prints for blocks, cut:

2 squares, 4¼" x 4¼" (112 total)

1 strip, 2" x 16" (56 total)

From *each* of the 56 light fabrics for blocks, cut:

2 squares, 4¼" x 4¼" (112 total)

1 strip, 2" x 16" (56 total)

1 square, 3½" x 3½" (56 total)

From the medium to dark scraps for sashing, cut a *total* of:

224 squares, 3½" x 3½" (56 matching sets of 4)

102 squares, 3½" x 3½"

From the light scraps for sashing, cut a *total* of:

112 rectangles, 3½" x 6½" (28 matching sets of 4)

15 rectangles, 3½" x 6½"

254 rectangles 2" x 3½"

From binding fabric, cut:

10 strips, 2½" x 42", *or* enough 2½" strips to total 386"

MAKING THE CHURN DASH BLOCKS

Refer to "Making the Churn Dash Blocks" on page 63 to make a total of 56 blocks.

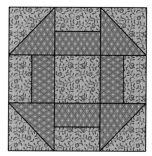

Make 56.

MAKING THE FLYING-GEESE AND SASHING UNITS

This quilt uses 127 flying-geese units. Of these, 112 are made in matching sets of four. The remaining 15 units will be separated in the body of the quilt and therefore don't need to match.

For each identical set of four you will need:
- 4 rectangles, 3½" x 6½" from one light fabric
- 4 squares, 3½" x 3½" from one medium to dark print
- 4 squares, 3½" x 3½" from a second medium to dark print

1. Choose the three fabrics that you want for a set of four flying-geese units. Fold each of the eight 3½" squares in half on the diagonal with *wrong sides together* and press.

Fold and crease.

2. Place four matching 3½" pressed squares right sides together on the left corner of four matching 3½" x 6½" rectangles as shown. Using the crease as a sewing line, sew one thread width outside the crease. Trim away the excess fabric ¼" beyond the line of stitching. Press to set the seam and press the seam allowances outward.

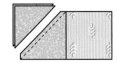

Make 4.

3. Repeat step 2 with the remaining four matching 3½" pressed squares, placing them on the right corner of each unit from step 2.

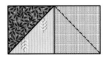

Make 4.

4. Repeat steps 1–3 until you have completed 28 matching sets of four flying-geese units. Then make an additional 15 flying-geese units; these do not need to be made in matching sets.

5. Make sashing units by sewing a 2" x 3½" rectangle to each end of a flying-geese unit as shown. The rectangles do not need to match. Press the seam allowances toward the rectangles. The units should measure 3½" x 9½".

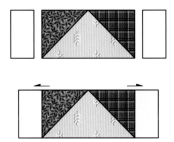

ASSEMBLING THE QUILT TOP

1. Working on your design wall and referring to the assembly diagram, arrange the Churn Dash blocks in eight horizontal rows of seven blocks each, leaving space for the sashing units and setting squares between blocks and rows. Frame alternate Churn Dash blocks (28) with a set of four matching sashing units. Choose sashing units with triangles that are of similar value or color to the background of the Churn Dash block. The long sides of the light sashing triangles should be adjacent to the Churn Dash block they surround.

2. Place the remaining 15 sashing units as needed around the edges of the quilt. Fill in the spaces with the medium to dark 3½" squares.

3. When you are happy with the arrangement, sew the blocks, sashing units, and squares together into rows. Press the seam allowances open. Join the rows, pressing the seam allowances open.

FINISHING THE QUILT

Refer to "Finishing the Quilt" on page 65 and layer the quilt so that the backing seams run horizontally. Join 2½" binding strips to total 386" and bind the quilt.

ALTERNATE CHURN DASH BLOCK LAYOUTS

CIVIL WAR AND BLUE

Made by Fran Urquhart.
Finished quilt: 76½" x 89½"
Finished block: 9" x 9"

Fran Urquhart used blue setting
blocks and a striking bias-cut striped
binding to set off her Churn Dash
blocks. This is the perfect way to get a
larger quilt with fewer pieced blocks.

I'LL FLY AWAY

Made by Barbara Reynolds.
Finished quilt: 100" x 115"
Finished block: 9" x 9"

Barbara Reynolds set her Churn
Dash blocks on point, side by side,
creating additional patterns and
interest. Notice her wonderful
pieced setting triangles—the strips
in the setting triangles align with the
seams of the Churn Dash blocks.
The border of flying geese provides
a dramatic frame.

CRISSCROSS

The light diagonal chain of small squares makes the Triple Four Patch block dramatic in many different settings. The fabric used for the chain needs to be lighter than any other fabrics used in the quilt.

For the trade, my group handed out one set of directions for the blocks, and then at a later date a slightly different version was provided. As a result, some blocks were made using three fabrics and some four. I think the difference in the blocks made more interesting quilts. The directions are for three fabrics but feel free to use an additional medium/dark for scrappier blocks.

MATERIALS

All yardages are based on 42"-wide fabric unless otherwise noted.

3¼ yards *total* of medium/dark scraps for blocks

1½ yards of gold print for border, corner blocks, and binding

1⅓ yards *total* of very light scraps for blocks

1⅓ yards *total* of very dark scraps for blocks

⅝ yard of dark green print for inner border and corner blocks

5½ yards of fabric for backing

66" x 90" piece of batting

CUTTING

All measurements include ¼"-wide seam allowances.

From the assorted medium/dark scraps, cut a total of:

192 squares, 3½" x 3½"*

384 squares, 2" x 2"*

From the very light scraps, cut:

96 strips, 1¼" x 12"

1 strip, 1¼" x 34"; crosscut into: 1 strip, 1¼" x 12" and 1 strip, 1¼" x 22" (set aside for the border corner blocks)

From the very dark scraps, cut:

96 strips, 1¼" x 12"

From the dark green print, cut:

1 strip, 1¼" x 22"

8 strips, 2" x 42"; crosscut 1 strip into 8 squares, 2" x 2"

From the gold print, cut:

1 strip, 1¼" x 12"

7 strips, 3½" x 42"

8 strips, 2½" x 42"

Cut two 3½" squares and four 2" squares from the same fabric to make 96 matching sets for blocks made of 3 fabrics. To use 4 fabrics, cut the four 2" squares from a different medium/dark.

CRISSCROSS
Made by Denise Goodman.
Finished quilt: 57½" x 81½" • Finished block: 6" x 6" • Number of blocks: 96

MAKING THE BLOCKS

There are two different Triple Four Patch blocks in the quilt. Block A uses three fabrics and Block B uses four. The instructions are written for making Block A. To make the scrappier Block B, simply substitute a different fabric for the 2" squares.

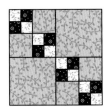 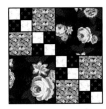

Block A   Block B

1. Sew a very light 1¼" x 12" strip to a very dark 1¼" x 12" strip along the long sides; press toward the dark fabric. Cut the strip set into eight 1¼" segments.

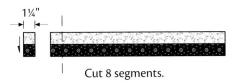

Cut 8 segments.

2. Pair the eight segments. Place each pair right sides together with seams butting as shown. Use a straight pin to secure the seams. Sew together and press the seam allowances open.

Make 4.

3. Arrange the four-patch units from step 2 with medium/dark 2" squares, as shown. Make certain the light squares are positioned correctly. Sew the pieces together into rows, and press the seam allowances toward the plain squares. Sew the rows together and press the seam allowances open. Make two.

Make 2.

4. Arrange the two double four-patch units from step 3 and the two matching medium/dark 3½" squares as shown. Make certain the light squares form a diagonal line. Sew together into rows and press the seam allowances toward the plain squares. Sew the rows together and press the seam allowances open.

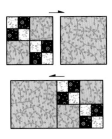 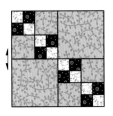

5. Repeat steps 1–4 to make a total of 96 blocks.

ASSEMBLING THE QUILT TOP

1. Working on a design wall, arrange the blocks in 12 horizontal rows of eight blocks each. Referring to the quilt diagram, rotate the blocks to form the diagonal pattern as shown.

2. Join the blocks together into rows. Press the seam allowances open. Join the rows, pressing the seam allowances open.

3. To make the four corner blocks for the dark green inner border, repeat steps 1 and 2 of "Making the Blocks" at left using a very light 1¼" x 12" strip and a gold 1¼" x 12" strip.

Make 4.

4. Sew two pairs of 2"-wide green strips end to end using a diagonal seam for the side inner borders. Press the seam allowances open. For the top and bottom, cut one of the 2"-wide green strips into two equal lengths and sew the half strips to each of the two remaining 42" green strips using a diagonal seam; press.

5. Referring to "Borders with Corner Squares" on page 22, add the inner borders using the gold Four Patch blocks made in step 3. Be certain the light squares are positioned as shown in the quilt diagram.

6. To make corner blocks for the outer border, repeat steps 1–3 using the very light 1¼" x 22" strip and the dark green 1¼" x 22" strip. Cut the strip set into 16 segments to make eight small Four Patch blocks. Arrange the Four Patch blocks with the 2" dark green squares to make the four corner blocks.

Make 4.

7. Sew two pairs of 3½"-wide gold strips together end to end using a diagonal seam for the side outer borders. Press the seam allowances open. Cut one of the 3½"-wide gold strips into two equal lengths. Using a diagonal seam, sew a half strip to each of the two remaining 42" gold strip for the top and bottom; press.

8. Referring to "Borders with Corner Squares" on page 22, add the outer borders using the green double Four Patch blocks from step 6. Be certain the light squares are positioned as shown in the quilt diagram.

FINISHING THE QUILT

1. Cut the backing fabric across the grain into two equal pieces. Remove the selvages. Sew these pieces together along the lengthwise grain to create the quilt back. Press the seam allowance open. The seam will run vertically on the quilt.

2. Refer to "Layering and Basting" on page 23; hand or machine quilt as desired.

3. Use the gold 2½"-strips to bind the quilt, referring to "Binding" on page 24.

4. Make and attach a label to your quilt.

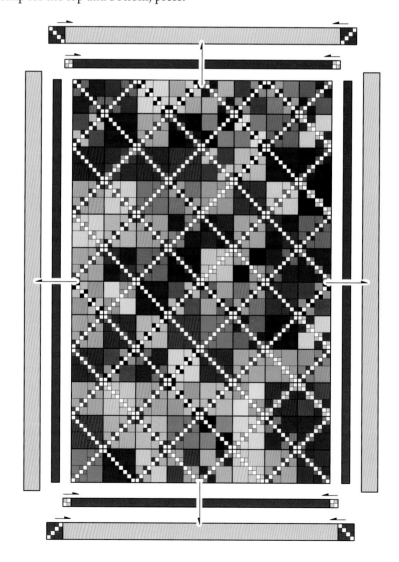

TRIPLE FOUR PATCH BLOCKS FOR TRADES

Finished size: 6" x 6" • Yield: 8

From very light fabric, cut:
2 strips, 1¼" x 42"

From very dark fabric, cut:
2 strips, 1¼" x 42"

From medium to dark fabric, cut:
2 strips, 2" x 42"; crosscut into 32 squares, 2" x 2"
2 strips, 3½" x 42"; crosscut into 16 squares, 3½" x 3½"

1. Sew each very light 1¼" x 42" strip to a very dark 1¼" x 42" strip along the long sides to make a strip set. Press the seam allowances toward the dark. Cut the strip set into 64 segments, 1¼" wide.

1¼"

Make 2 strip sets.
Cut 64 segments.

2. Pair the segments and place each pair right sides together with seams butting. Use a straight pin to secure the seams. Sew together and press the seam allowances open.

Make 32.

3. Arrange the 32 four-patch units from step 2, and 32 medium to dark 2" squares *exactly* as shown. Sew together and press the seam allowances toward the plain squares.

Make 32.

4. Pair the units from step 3. Sew together to form 16 double four-patch units. Press the seam allowances open.

Make 16.

5. Arrange the 16 double four-patch units from step 4 and 16 medium to dark 3½" squares, *exactly* as shown. Sew together and press the seam allowances toward the plain squares.

  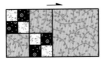

Make 16.

6. Pair 16 units from step 3 and sew together to form 8 Triple Four Patch blocks. Press the seam allowances open.

  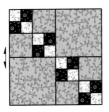

Make 8.

UFO COMPLETE
Made by Betty Rivers. Machine quilted by Jane Plisga.
Finished quilt: 63½" x 87½" • Finished block: 6" x 6" • Number of blocks: 90

UFO COMPLETE

In this quilt, the small light squares of the Triple Four Patch block create a delightful woven effect. The quilt looks difficult but is actually easy to piece in vertical rows.

My group traded these blocks in 1997. With this book deadline as motivation, Betty completed her UFO (unfinished object) 10 years later.

MATERIALS

All yardages are based on 42"-wide fabric unless otherwise noted.

5½ yards *total* of medium/dark scraps for blocks and plain squares

1¼ yards *total* of very light scraps for blocks

1¼ yards *total* of very dark scraps for blocks

⅔ yard of dark purple fabric for binding

5⅞ yards of fabric for backing

72" x 96" piece of batting

CUTTING

All measurements include ¼"-wide seam allowances.

From the assorted medium/dark scraps, cut a *total* of:

180 squares, 3½" x 3½"*

360 squares, 2" x 2"*

10 squares, 2" x 2"**

244 squares, 3½" x 3½"

From the very light scraps, cut:

90 strips, 1¼" x 12"

5 strips, 1¼" x 6"

From the very dark scraps, cut:

90 strips, 1¼" x 12"

5 strips, 1¼" x 6"

From the dark purple fabric cut:

8 strips, 2½" x 42"

*Cut two 3½" squares and four 2" squares from the same fabric to make 90 matching sets for blocks made of 3

fabrics. To use 4 fabrics, cut the four 2" squares from a different medium/dark fabric.

**Cut two squares from the same fabric to make 5 matching pairs.

MAKING THE BLOCKS

1. Refer to "Making the Blocks" on page 73 and follow steps 1–4 to make a total of 90 Triple Four Patch blocks.

Make 90.

2. To make Double Four Patch blocks for the left side of the quilt, follow steps 1–3 of "Making the Blocks" on page 73 using the very light 1¼" x 6" strips and very dark 1¼" x 6" strips, and cutting the strip sets into four 1¼" segments. Use the five matching pairs of 2" squares and make a total of 5 blocks.

Make 5.

3. Pair 220 of the 3½" squares using fabrics that contrast in color or value. Sew the pairs together to make 110 double-square units. Press the seam allowances open.

Make 110.

ASSEMBLING THE QUILT TOP

1. The quilt is pieced together in 11 vertical rows or panels. Refer to the quilt assembly diagram and arrange the units on your design wall as indicated below. Make certain the pieced blocks are positioned correctly. Rearrange units or blocks until you are pleased with the composition.

Panel 1: 5 Double Four Patch blocks and 24 single 3½" squares

Panels 2, 4, 6, 8 and 10: 9 Triple Four Patch blocks and 11 double-square units

Panels 3, 5, 7 and 9: 10 Triple Four Patch blocks and 9 double-square units

Panel 11: 5 Triple Four Patch blocks and 19 double-square units

2. Join the units in the first vertical row. Press the seam allowances of the Double Four Patch blocks toward a plain square. Press the remaining seam allowances open.

3. Join the units in rows 2, 4, 6, 8, and 10. Press the seam allowances of the Triple Four Patch blocks toward the double-square units. Press the remaining seam allowance open.

4. Join the units in rows 3, 5, 7 and 9. Press the seam allowances of the Triple Four Patch blocks toward the double-square units.

5. Join the units in row 11. Press the seam allowances of the Triple Four Patch blocks toward the double-square units. Press the remaining seam allowances open.

6. Join the vertical rows. Press the seam allowances open.

FINISHING THE QUILT

1. Cut the backing fabric across the grain into two equal pieces. Remove the selvages. Sew these pieces together along the lengthwise grain to create the quilt back. Press the seam allowance open. The seam will run vertically on the quilt.

2. Refer to "Layering and Basting" on page 23; hand or machine quilt as desired.

3. Use the dark purple 2½"-strips to bind the quilt, referring to "Binding" on page 24.

4. Make and attach a label to your quilt.

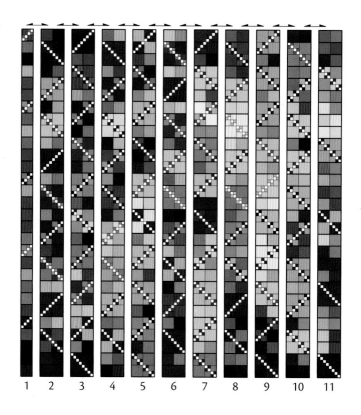

1 2 3 4 5 6 7 8 9 10 11

ALTERNATE TRIPLE FOUR PATCH BLOCK LAYOUT

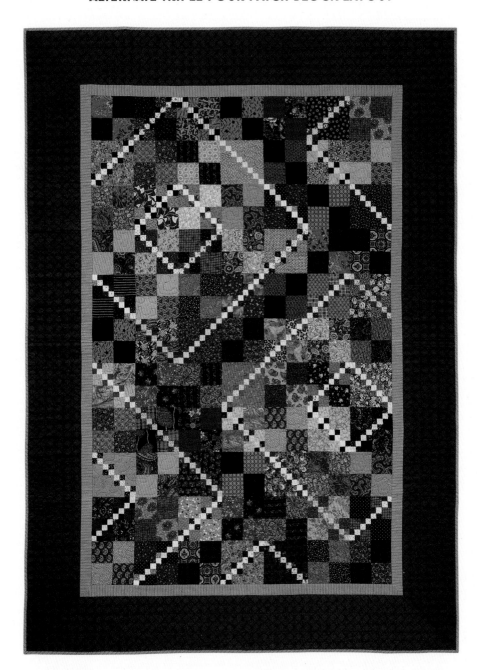

THE "UGLY FABRIC" QUILT

Made by Lynn Roddy Brown.
Finished quilt: 60" x 84" • Finished block: 6" x 6"

I traded 28 Triple Four Patch blocks. I pieced a few more Triple Four Patch blocks and then added several of the much easier, large Four Patch blocks. When I was designing the quilt, I envisioned a tile floor. I told myself that if I had taken a photo of the floor, the squares on the floor wouldn't be evenly framed in the photograph. Even though the pattern in this quilt is incomplete, you know what it should be.

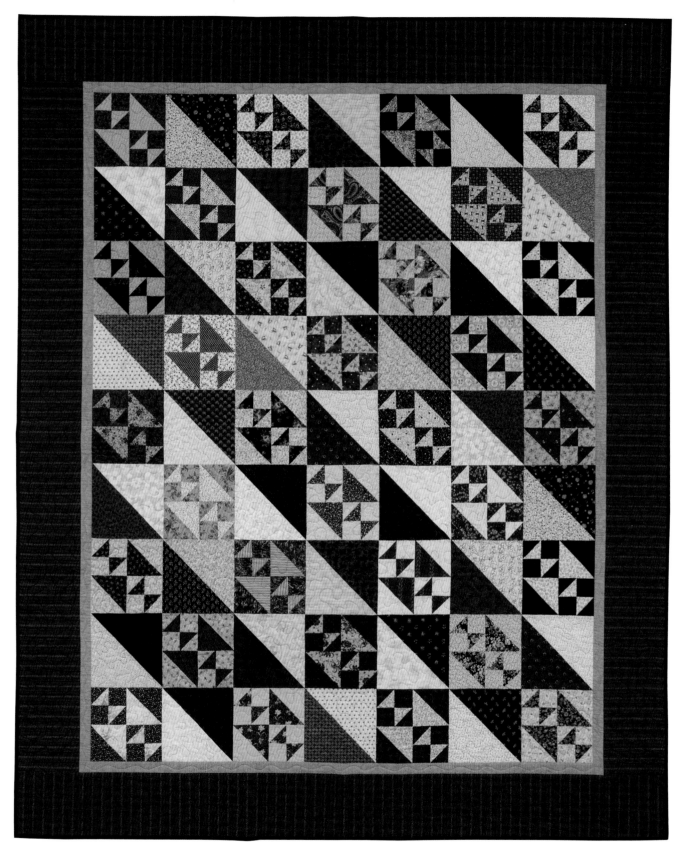

GOOSE THE FOX
Made by Lynn Roddy Brown.
Finished quilt: 73" x 89" • Finished block: 8" x 8" • Number of blocks: 32

GOOSE THE FOX

When my group traded the Fox and Geese blocks, the instructions stated that each block should use one light and one medium to dark fabric. We could decide the position of the values within the blocks. Working on my design wall, I arranged the blocks in diagonal rows determined by the value of the backgrounds. When I added the alternate blocks, I placed the light side next to a darker Fox and Geese background.

Look carefully at the purple Fox and Geese block in the top row, and you will notice one on the smaller units turned the wrong way. I made this block and put it in our trade. Luckily it came back to me. I decided this was a sign that I needed to be less controlling and used the block.

MATERIALS

All yardages are based on 42"-wide fabric unless otherwise noted.

2⅛ yards *total* of assorted fabrics for Fox and Geese blocks background (fabric B)

1⅞ yards of purple striped fabric for outer border

1½ yards *total* of assorted fabrics for Fox and Geese blocks (fabric A)

½ yard of pink tone-on-tone fabric for inner border

16 squares, 9½" x 9½", of assorted light prints for alternate blocks

16 squares, 9½" x 9½", of assorted medium to dark prints for alternate blocks

¾ yard of dark purple print for binding

6 yards of fabric for backing

81" x 97" piece of batting

CUTTING

All measurements include ¼"-wide seam allowances.

From the A fabrics, cut a *total* of:
32 squares, 5¼" x 5¼"*
64 squares, 3¼" x 3¼"*

From the B fabrics, cut a *total* of:
32 squares, 5¼" x 5¼"**
64 squares, 3¼" x 3¼"**
128 squares, 2½" x 2½"**

From the pink tone-on-tone fabric, cut:
8 strips, 1¾" x 42"

From the purple striped fabric, cut:
8 strips, 7½" x 42"

From the dark purple print, cut:
9 strips, 2½" x 42"

Cut one 5¼" square and two 3¼" squares from the same fabric.
**Cut one 5¼" square, two 3¼" squares and four 2½" squares from the same fabric.*

MAKING THE BLOCKS

The quilt as shown has 16 blocks with light backgrounds and 16 blocks with medium to dark backgrounds. For each block, choose one A and one B fabric.

• From fabric A, you will need: 1 square, 5¼" x 5¼" and 2 squares, 3¼" x 3¼"

• From fabric B, you will need: 1 square, 5¼" x 5¼"; 2 squares, 3¼" x 3¼"; and 4 squares, 2½" x 2½"

Fabric A

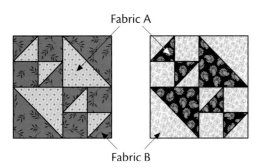

Fabric B

1. Pair the 3¼" squares of fabrics A and B together. Referring to "Half-Square-Triangle Units" on page 18, make two units. Press the seam allowances toward the medium to dark fabric and trim to 2½" square.

2. Using the four half-square-triangle units from step 1 and four 2½" squares of fabric B, arrange the pieces as shown. Make certain the half-square-triangle units are positioned correctly. Sew the pieces together into rows and press the seam allowances toward the plain squares. Sew the rows together and press the seam allowances open.

Make 2.

3. Pair the 5¼" squares of fabrics A and B together and repeat step 1. Trim the units to 4½" square.

4. Arrange the units created in step 2 and the two half-square-triangle units from step 3 as shown. *Make certain all of the units are positioned correctly.* Sew the pieces together into rows and press the seam allowances open. Sew the rows together and press the seam allowances open.

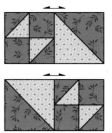 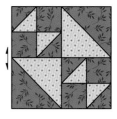

5. Repeat steps 1–4 to make 32 blocks.

6. Pair each light 9½" square with a medium to dark 9½" square to make two half-square-triangle units from each. Make a total of 32. Press the seam allowances toward the medium to dark fabric and trim completed units to 8½" square. You will have one extra block.

ASSEMBLING THE QUILT TOP

1. Referring to the quilt diagram, arrange the Fox and Geese and half-square-triangle blocks on a design wall in nine horizontal rows of seven blocks each, alternating the blocks as shown. I alternated the Fox and Geese blocks in diagonal rows, based on the value of the backgrounds. The light side of each half-square triangle is next to a Fox and Geese block with a dark background.

2. When you are happy with the arrangement, join the blocks to form rows. Press the seam allowances open. Join the rows and press the seam allowances open.

3. Sew the pink 1¾"-wide strips together in pairs end to end using a diagonal seam. Referring to "Borders with Butted Corners" on page 21, add the side borders and then the top and bottom borders. Press the seam allowances toward the borders.

4. Sew the purple striped 7½"-wide strips together in pairs end to end, matching the stripes and joining using a straight seam. Make four border strips. Press the seam allowances open. Add the side borders and press the seam allowances toward the borders. Add the top and bottom borders and press.

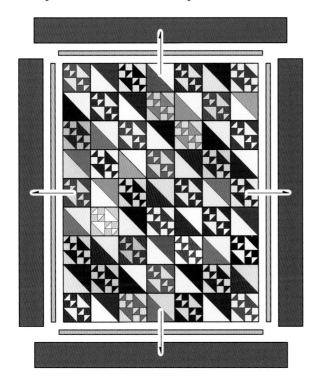

FINISHING THE QUILT

1. Cut the backing fabric across the grain into two equal pieces. Remove the selvages. Sew these pieces together along the lengthwise grain to create the quilt back. Press the seam allowance open. The seam will run vertically on the quilt.

2. Refer to "Layering and Basting" on page 23; hand or machine quilt as desired.

3. Use the dark purple 2½" strips to bind the quilt, referring to "Binding" on page 24.

4. Make and attach a label to your quilt.

FOX AND GEESE BLOCKS FOR TRADES

Finished size: 8" x 8" • Yield: 6

From the fox and geese fabric (A), cut:
1 strip, 5¼" x 42"; crosscut into 6 squares, 5¼" x 5¼"
1 strip, 3¼" x 42"; crosscut into 12 squares, 3¼" x 3¼"

From the background fabric (B), cut:
1 strip, 5¼" x 42"; crosscut into 6 squares, 5¼" x 5¼"
1 strip, 3¼" x 42"; crosscut into 12 squares, 3¼" x 3¼"
2 strips, 2½" x 42"; crosscut into 24 squares, 2½" x 2½

1. Pair the 3¼" squares of fabric A and B together, referring to "Half-Square-Triangle Units" on page 18. Make two identical units from each pair. Press the seam allowances toward the medium to dark fabric and trim completed units to 2½" square. Make a total of 24 units.

2. Arrange two half-square-triangle units and two 2½" squares of fabric B as shown. Make certain the half-square-triangle units are positioned correctly. Sew into rows and press the seam allowances toward the plain squares. Sew the rows together and press the seam allowances open.

Make 12.

3. Repeat step 1, pairing the 5¼" squares of fabric A and B. Trim the completed units to 4½" square. Make a total of 12 units.

4. Arrange the units from step 2 and half-square-triangle units from step 3 as shown. *Make certain all of the units are positioned correctly.* Sew together into rows and press the seam allowances open. Sew the rows together and press the seam allowance open.

  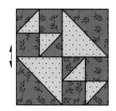

Make 6.

ORANGE CAN BE WONDERFUL
Made by Lynn Roddy Brown.

Finished quilt: 63" x 77" • Finished block: 8" x 8" • Number of blocks: 18

ORANGE CAN BE WONDERFUL

This quilt is one of my second-chance quilts. The blocks were left over from "Goose the Fox" on page 81. The orange plaid and black floral block (third position in the first vertical row) didn't seem to go with any of the other blocks. I applied the "take it out or add more" rule and made two additional blocks using orange. Then I chose reddish orange setting triangles. Instead of being set aside, the block drove the design of the quilt. To help balance the bright colors and strong visual textures of the blocks, I separated them with a calm sashing. I love getting two entirely different quilts from one block trade.

MATERIALS

All yardages are based on 42"-wide fabric unless otherwise noted.

2 yards of navy floral for outer border

1⅔ yards of red-orange print for setting triangles and binding

1⅛ yards of dark gray tone-on-tone fabric for sashing

1⅛ yards *total* of assorted fabrics for Fox and Geese blocks background (fabric B)

⅞ yard *total* of assorted fabrics for Fox and Geese blocks (fabric A)

⅜ yard of yellow print for inner border

5¼ yards of fabric for backing

71" x 85" piece of batting

CUTTING

All measurements include ¼"-wide seam allowances.

From the A fabrics, cut a *total* of:

18 squares, 5¼" x 5¼"*

36 squares, 3¼" x 3¼"*

From the B fabrics, cut a *total* of:

18 squares, 5¼" x 5¼"**

36 squares, 3¼" x 3¼"**

72 squares, 2½" x 2½"**

From the dark gray tone-on-tone fabric, cut:

14 strips, 2½" x 42"; cut 9 strips into:†

    24 strips, 2½" x 8½"

    2 strips, 2½" x 12½"

    2 strips, 2½" x 32½"

From the red-orange print, cut:

3 squares, 16½" x 16½"; cut each square twice diagonally to yield 12 side triangles (2 are extra).

2 squares, 10½" x 10½"; cut each square once diagonally to yield 4 corner triangles.

8 strips, 2½" x 42"

From the yellow print, cut:

7 strips, 1½" x 42"

From the navy floral, cut:

4 strips, 8" x 66", from the *lengthwise* grain

Cut one 5¼" square and two 3¼" squares from the same fabric.

**Cut one 5¼" square, two 3¼" squares and four 2½" squares from the same fabric.*

†*Wait until the blocks are completed to cut the sashing strips.*

MAKING THE BLOCKS

The blocks have both light and dark backgrounds. Feel free to make some of both or all of one type. Refer to "Making the Blocks" on page 82 to make 18 Fox and Geese blocks.

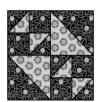

Make 18.

ASSEMBLING THE QUILT TOP

The Fox and Geese blocks should measure 8½" x 8½"; the lengths of the sashing strips in the steps that follow are based on 8½" blocks. If your blocks don't measure 8½", you'll need to measure and adjust the length that you cut *all* of the sashing strips.

1. Referring to the quilt diagram, arrange the blocks and the gray 2½" x 8½" sashing strips on a design wall in diagonal rows. When you are happy with block placement, sew the blocks and sashing strips in diagonal rows. Press the seam allowances toward the sashing.

2. Cut and piece the remaining 2½" sashing strips together with a diagonal seam. Press the seam allowances open. Cut strips as follows (or measure the rows and use your measurements): 2 strips, 2½" x 52½" and 1 strip, 2½" x 62½".

3. Add the 12½", 32½", and 52½" sashing strips to the design wall. Referring to "Diagonal Sets" on page 21, join the block rows and sashing. Press the seam allowances toward the sashing. Add the orange side triangles and press seam allowances toward the triangles.

4. Add the 62½" sashing strip and sew the rows together. Add the corner triangles last. Press the seam allowance toward the sashing.

5. Trim the quilt on all four sides, leaving a ¼" seam allowance beyond the points of the sashing.

6. Sew four yellow 1½"-wide strips together in pairs end to end using a diagonal seam to make the side inner borders. Press this seam allowance open. To make the top and bottom inner borders, cut one of the 1½"-wide yellow strips into two equal lengths. Sew a half strip to each remaining 42" strip using a diagonal seam.

7. Referring to "Borders with Butted Corners" on page 21, add the side inner borders. Press the seam allowance toward the borders. Add the top and bottom inner borders and press.

8. Repeat to add the navy floral outer borders in the same manner.

FINISHING THE QUILT

1. Cut the backing fabric across the grain into two equal pieces. Remove the selvages. Sew these pieces together along the lengthwise grain to create the quilt back. Press the seam allowance open. The seam will run vertically on the quilt.

2. Refer to "Layering and Basting" on page 23; hand or machine quilt as desired.

3. Use the red-orange 2½"-strips to bind the quilt, referring to "Binding" on page 24.

4. Make and attach a label to your quilt.

ALTERNATE FOX AND GEESE BLOCK LAYOUTS

QUILTED RAINBOW

Made by Fran Urquhart.
Machine quilted by Sharon Dixon.
Finished quilt: 78½" x 102½"
Finished block: 8" x 8"

Fran Urquhart alternated light backgrounds with dark backgrounds, and then turned the blocks so hourglass shapes formed where the blocks meet. One of Fran's favorite ways to sort blocks is by color. She started with red blocks in the upper-left corner and changed colors as she moved across and down the quilt. This gorgeous, scrappy quilt is one of my favorites.

BOUNCING BETTY

Made by Betty Rivers.
Finished quilt: 56½" x 68"
Finished block: 8" x 8"

Another name for the Fox and Geese block is Bouncing Betty. For some reason, Betty Rivers liked this name for her quilt. Betty's quilt, like "Goose the Fox" on page 81, uses a large half-square-triangle unit as the alternate block but she put her blocks on point and made use of her stash of striped fabrics. Notice that the stripes in each vertical row are the same fabric. This is an example of what I call underlying structure.

TIPSY NINE PATCH
Made by Lynn Roddy Brown.
Finished quilt: 68½" x 84½" • Finished block: 8½" x 8½" • Number of blocks: 48

TIPSY NINE PATCH

In the Crossroads to Jericho trade, my group used tone-on-tone black fabrics for the nine-patch units. The tone-on-tone fabrics create a strong line that unifies the quilt.

Once I decided on the light blue fabric for the inner border of this quilt, I made two additional blocks with light blue fabric for a total of five. Odd numbers seem to work best with strong colors or those you want to emphasize. The all-black outer border I had planned overpowered the quilt. This was a case of thinking I knew what I was going to do before I had the blocks on my design wall. As a result, I learned to make dogtooth borders.

MATERIALS

All yardages are based on 42"-wide fabric unless otherwise noted.

3⅓ yards *total* of assorted prints that contrast with black for blocks

2⅛ yards of tone-on-tone black fabric 1 for blocks and pieced border*

¾ yard of tone-on-tone black fabric 2 for outer border

⅔ yard of light blue fabric for inner border

⅝ yard of medium blue fabric for pieced border

⅔ yards of tone-on-tone black fabric 3 for binding

5⅔ yards of fabric for backing

76" x 93" piece of batting

*Since my blocks came from a trade, there were many different tone-on-tone black fabrics. I used an assortment of black fabrics for the pieced border. You might want to substitute 9 fat quarters for the black fabric 1 yardage.

CUTTING

All measurements include ¼"-wide seam allowances.

From the assorted prints, cut a *total* of:

96 squares, 5½" x 5½"; cut each square once diagonally to make 192 triangles*

192 squares, 2½" x 2½"*

From the tone-on-tone black fabric 1, cut:

16 strips, 2½" x 42"; crosscut into 240 squares 2½" x 2½"

3 strips, 9¼" x 42"; crosscut into 9 squares, 9¼" x 9¼". Cut 7 squares twice diagonally to yield 28 side triangles. Cut 2 squares once diagonally to yield 4 corner triangles.

From medium blue fabric, cut:

2 strips, 9¼" x 42"; crosscut into 8 squares, 9¼" x 9¼". Cut each square twice diagonally to yield 32 side triangles.

From light blue fabric, cut:

4 strips, 3" x 42"

3 strips, 2½" x 42"

From tone-on-tone black fabric 2, cut:

9 strips, 2½" x 42"

From tone-on-tone black fabric 3, cut:

8 strips, 2½" x 42"

*Cut one 5½" square and two 2½" squares from the same fabric.

MAKING THE BLOCKS

1. Select five black 2½" squares and four assorted 2½" squares. Arrange the squares in rows as shown and sew the rows together. Press the seam allowances toward the black squares. Sew the top and bottom rows to the center row, matching seams. Press the seam allowances open.

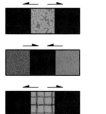

2. Sew the matching half-square triangles to the nine-patch unit as shown, referring to "Square-in-a-Square Units" on page 19. Press away from the center. Trim the block to 9" x 9".

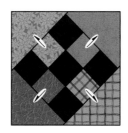

3. Repeat steps 1 and 2 to make a total of 48 blocks.

ASSEMBLING THE QUILT TOP

1. Working on a design wall, arrange the blocks in eight horizontal rows of six blocks each. Move blocks around until you are pleased with the arrangement. Sew the blocks into rows and press the seam allowances open. Join the rows and press seam allowances open.

2. Sew four light blue 3"-wide strips together end to end in pairs using a diagonal seam for each of the side borders. Press the seam allowances open. Referring to "Borders with Butted Corners" on page 21, add the side inner borders. Press the seam allowances toward the borders.

3. To make the top and bottom inner borders, cut one light blue 2½"-wide strip into two equal lengths; sew a half strip to each of the remaining 2½" x 42" strips using a diagonal seam. Press the seam allowances

open. Add the top and bottom inner borders and press the seam allowances toward the borders.

4. Sewing the triangles for the pieced border is much easier if the triangle points are trimmed. To trim the points, you can use a special point trimmer ruler or a rotary ruler with ⅛" marks. Align the ⅜" line with a short edge of the triangle. Position the ruler so the corner is just touching the long edge of the triangle as shown. Trim the point. Rotate the triangle and trim the second point. Repeat for all 32 blue triangles and 28 black triangles.

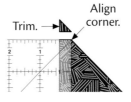

5. Each pieced border starts and ends with a medium blue triangle. To join the border triangles, place a medium blue triangle right sides together with a black triangle as shown. Notice the position of the ¼" seam line in relation to the trimmed point. Sew the seam and press open. Join seven blue triangles and six black triangles for the top and bottom borders. Piece the side borders, each having nine blue triangles and eight black triangles.

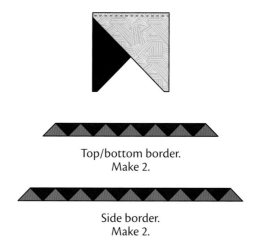

Top/bottom border.
Make 2.

Side border.
Make 2.

6. Add the side borders using pins and a steam iron if necessary to adjust the fit. Press the seam allowances toward the light blue border. Add the top and bottom borders. Press the seam allowances toward the light blue border. Add the corner triangles and press outward.

7. Sew the 2½"-wide black fabric 2 outer border strips together in pairs end to end using a diagonal seam. Press the seam allowances open. Cut an additional strip into two equal lengths and sew a half strip to the end of two of the long strips using diagonal seams, to make side outer borders. Press the seam allowances open.

8. Add the black fabric 2 outer borders and press seam allowances open.

FINISHING THE QUILT

1. Cut the backing fabric across the grain into two equal pieces. Remove the selvages. Sew these pieces together along the lengthwise grain to create the quilt back. Press the seam allowance open. The seam will run vertically on the quilt.

2. Refer to "Layering and Basting" on page 23; hand or machine quilt as desired.

3. Use the 2½" strips of black fabric 3 to bind the quilt, referring to "Binding" on page 24.

4. Make and attach a label to your quilt.

CROSSROADS TO JERICHO BLOCKS FOR TRADES

Finished size: 8½" x 8½" • Yield: 6

From a tone-on-tone black fabric, cut:
5 strips, 2½" x 16"

From *each* of 4 different fabrics that contrast with black, cut:
1 strip, 2½" x 16" (4 total)
3 squares, 5½" x 5½"; cut the squares once diagonally to make 6 triangles (24 total)

1. Make three strip sets as shown. Press toward the black. Cut each strip set into six 2½" segments.

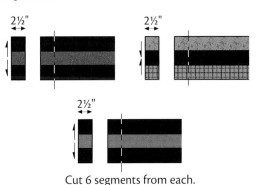

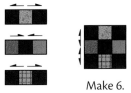

Cut 6 segments from each.

2. Arrange one segment from each strip set as shown. Sew the side units to the center unit, matching seams. Press the seam allowances open. Repeat until you have made six blocks.

Make 6.

3. Match each of the triangles to a square in a Nine Patch block. Refer to "Square-in-a-Square Units" on page 19. Join the triangles to each of the blocks and trim to 8½" x 8½".

Make 6.

WHICH WAY DID HE GO?
Made by Barbara Reynolds.
Finished quilt: 73½" x 85½" • Finished block: 8½" x 8½" • Number of blocks: 50

WHICH WAY DID HE GO?

When we did this trade, one member brought blocks with very clear, bright fabrics. I immediately decided that the blocks were for two different quilts and traded away my bright blocks. Barbara Reynolds used all of her blocks and added more bright fabrics in the pieced setting triangles. We both used the "add more or take it out" approach. Barbara added more with wonderful results.

MATERIALS

All yardages are based on 42"-wide fabric unless otherwise noted.

4 yards *total* of assorted fabrics that contrast with black for blocks and setting triangles

2⅜ yards of black-and-red print for outer border

1⅜ yards of medium gray print for setting triangles

1⅓ yards of black tone-on-tone fabric for blocks

¾ yard of fabric for binding*

5¾ yards of fabric for backing

82" x 94" piece of batting

Barbara made a pieced binding from assorted 2½"-strips of different lengths. For a scrappy binding, use coordinating scraps from your stash.

CUTTING

All measurements include ¼"-wide seam allowances.

From assorted fabrics, cut a *total* of:

100 squares, 5½" x 5½"; cut each square once diagonally to yield 200 triangles*

200 squares, 2½" x 2½"*

9 squares, 5¼" x 5¼"; cut each square once diagonally to yield 18 triangles

From black tone-on-tone fabric, cut:

17 strips, 2½" x 42"; crosscut into 250 squares, 2½" x 2½"

From medium gray print, cut:

9 strips, 3¾" x 42"; crosscut into 18 strips, 3¾" x 14½"

2 squares, 8" x 8"; cut once diagonally to yield 4 corner setting triangles

From black-and-red print, cut:

4 strips, 7" x 78", from the *lengthwise* grain

From binding fabric, cut:

9 strips, 2½" x 42" **OR** 2½" strips in random lengths to total 330"

Cut one 5½" square, and two 2½" squares from the same fabric.

MAKING BLOCKS

Referring to "Making the Blocks" on page 90, make 50 Crossroads to Jericho blocks.

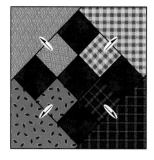

Make 50.

MAKING SIDE SETTING TRIANGLES

1. Mark the center of each long side of the 18 medium gray 3¾" x 14½" strips by folding in half right sides together and lightly pressing. Fold the 18 triangles cut from 5¼" squares of assorted prints with wrong sides together; mark the center of each long edge by lightly pressing. Lay each triangle on a strip, right sides together, matching the center creases. Stitch as shown. Press the seam allowances toward the gray strips.

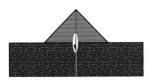

2. Lay a ruler along one pieced triangle edge as shown and trim the excess gray fabric. Repeat for the opposite side. The long edge of the pieced triangle should measure between 13¾" and 14". Trim all of the triangle units from step 1.

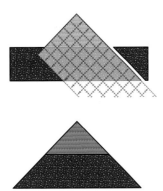

ASSEMBLING THE QUILT TOP

1. Referring to the quilt diagram, arrange the blocks and the side setting triangles in diagonal rows on a design wall.

2. Referring to "Diagonal Sets" on page 21, join the blocks into rows. Join the setting triangles to the rows making certain that the pieced triangle seams align with the block seam. Press the seam allowances open. Trim the point of the triangle as shown, and trim the opposite edge as well, if needed.

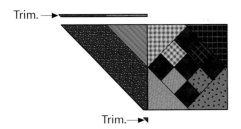

Trim.

Trim.

3. Join the rows and press the seam allowances open. Add the corner setting triangles. Press outward. Trim and square up the quilt on all four sides, leaving a ¼" seam allowance beyond the points of the blocks.

4. Referring to "Borders with Butted Corners" on page 21 and using the black-and-red 7" strips, add the side borders. Press the seam allowances toward the borders. Add the top and bottom borders and press.

FINISHING THE QUILT

1. Cut the backing fabric across the grain into two equal pieces. Remove the selvages. Sew these pieces together along the lengthwise grain to create the quilt back. Press the seam allowance open. The seam will run vertically on the quilt.

2. Refer to "Layering and Basting" on page 23; hand or machine quilt as desired.

3. Use 2½" strips of your fabric choice for binding or, for a scrappy binding, join 2½" strips of random lengths. You will need 330" of binding. Refer to "Binding" on page 24.

4. Make and attach a label to your quilt.

DOUBLE DIZZY WEDDING

Made by Elizabeth (Liz) Broussard.
Finished quilt size: 46" x 56"

Liz's solution for some trades is to just "cut the blocks into submission." For this quilt, she used a set of Double Wedding Ring templates. Look closely to see what remains of the Crossroads to Jericho blocks inside the rings. This is another solution for blocks that aren't the same size.

ABOUT THE AUTHOR

Lynn Roddy Brown is a sixth generation Texan who has always loved to sew. She took her first sewing lessons at the age of eight at the local Singer sewing-machine shop. When she was 10, she won the Singer regional dressmaking contest and received a sewing machine as her prize.

As she was growing up, there was one beautiful quilt in her home, made by Lynn's great grandmother as a wedding gift for her parents. This quilt, which now belongs to Lynn, kindled a lifelong interest in quilting. In the early 1970s, she began tearing pictures of quilts from magazines and did some patchwork with templates, but it was not until 1989 when she lived in Rochester, New York, that she began to quilt seriously.

For the past 10 years, she has been a member of a bee that trades blocks for scrap quilts. She loves scrap quilts because they give her the opportunity to use many different fabrics. She has had three of her quilts hung in the IQA juried show in Houston, Texas, two of which were scrap quilts. Her first book, *Simple Strategies for Scrap Quilts* (Martingale & Company), was published in 2006.

Lynn currently lives in Houston, Texas, with her husband, an economics professor at Rice University. She and her husband have also lived in Pennsylvania, New Jersey, and New York. They have three grown children (Kim, Wes, and Nancy), one wonderful son-in-law (Craig), and two cherished grandchildren (Lillian and Eli). Lynn has been a seventh-grade science teacher and computer programmer. She received a kidney transplant in January of 2002, for which she is truly grateful.